A Month of Comfort and Wisdom

A Month of Comfort and Wisdom

Five-Minute Meditations for Fresh Spiritual Strength

W. DOUGLAS HOOD JR.
MICHAEL B. BROWN
Includes Daily Prayers by LEO S. THORNE

Foreword by Thomas K. Tewell

WIPF & STOCK · Eugene, Oregon

A MONTH OF COMFORT AND WISDOM
Five-Minute Meditations for Fresh Spiritual Strength

Wipf & Stock
An Imprint of Wipf and Stock Publishers
199 W. 8th Ave., Suite 3
Eugene, OR 97401

www.wipfandstock.com

PAPERBACK ISBN: 979-8-3852-8047-6
HARDCOVER ISBN: 979-8-3852-8048-3
EBOOK ISBN: 979-8-3852-8049-0

Contents

Foreword

In the spring of 2024, I accepted a ten-week preaching engagement at a church in Birmingham, Alabama. I had not preached ten Sundays in a row in several years, so it was an exciting and yet scary experience for me. But as I got back into the pulpit every week, I *loved* it! I thoroughly enjoyed the weekly preparation of researching, writing, and delivering ten different sermons. One of the things that I most loved about the experience was preaching to the same congregation week after week. I got to know the individual people and their families. I got to know their joys and sorrows, challenges and disappointments. I got to know how they expressed their faith and their questions about God. It was a privilege for me to gain the trust of the congregation. I loved being with them during the week and every Sunday, too. I loved being their pastor!

One of the spiritual practices that I started in that Birmingham congregation was "homework" every week in the bulletin. I took the entire back page of the bulletin and offered a Scripture passage, reflection questions, challenges for living, and a prayer assignment for each day of that coming week. I asked everyone in the congregation to *join me* in setting aside ten minutes per day for God. I was amazed with the response! Many in the congregation not only joined me but also wrote me notes about how this practice deepened their spiritual lives. The thing they kept saying repeatedly is that once they got into *the habit* of daily Scripture reading, prayer, and reflection . . . they *wanted* to continue! People told me that they continued the habit after my ten weeks were over.

Early in my ministry, I learned the importance of cultivating daily habits when a member of the first congregation I served gave me a copy of Oswald Chambers' classic *My Utmost for His Highest*. I savored each daily devotional as if it was manna from heaven. It was! Chambers was a Scotsman who wrote in the late nineteenth and early twentieth century. In his daily devotional writings, he urged his readers to come before God for a regular time of reflection, Scripture, and prayer *each day*! Chambers believed that our daily habits of heart, mind, and soul shape our character. Chambers wanted people to go before God daily and to cultivate habits that would bear fruit in daily living and give them comfort and strength amid the vicissitudes of daily life. He believed with all his heart that people needed to seek God daily. This is why he said, "It is spiritual lust to seek answers from God instead of seeking God who is our answer."[1] Chambers wanted his readers to seek God *alone* for the strength to carry on each day.

In many ways, my two dear friends, Doug Hood and Michael Brown, are "the Oswald Chambers of the twenty-first century." As you will read in Doug's preface, these two seasoned pastors and preachers do not want us to read this book in one sitting or even in a few sittings. The key is the *daily* walk with God. They urge us to spend ten minutes a day: five in reading the material, and five in prayer and reflecting on what we have read. They urge us to resist the impulse to get the book finished. It is not meant to be finished! Instead, the habits we will cultivate are meant to last a lifetime.

Doug and Michael hope for nothing less than that this spiritual discipline will give us access to the real source of comfort and strength . . . God. They would counsel us that only Jesus Christ can satisfy the deepest longing and assuage the deepest thirst of our soul. They want us to learn this truth so that when we face a challenge, a deep hurt, a time of grief or loss, or when we are disappointed and feel anger, resentment, and bitterness . . . we will get in the habit of going to God, *the true source of comfort and strength*.

I was invited back to preach recently in the church I served in Birmingham almost a year after my ten weeks were over. I was

1. Chambers, *My Utmost*, February 7.

amazed at how many people told me that the thing they missed the most after I left the church was the homework! So . . . they made up their own homework and they continued to read Scripture, pray, and reflect *every day* as I invited them to do the year before. And they discovered that the habit of seeking God daily provided the strength they need to live in these tumultuous times.

The book you have in your hands is a treasure. I should know. I have been reading it one devotion a day for thirty-one days. If you will join me in reading one of these devotions *each day* I believe with all my heart that *we* will meet the God who provides the comfort and wisdom that *only* God can give! May it be so!

With joy in the daily adventure ahead of us,

Rev. Dr. Tom Tewell

Preface

SOMEONE WISER THAN I once said, "Change your focus, change your reality."[1] What Michael Brown and I hope to do with the publication of this small volume is come alongside people who face difficulties, obstacles, and a general mood of self-defeat. We seek to help redirect their focus upon God and the tremendous resources of our faith so that reality is changed. Often in our ministry, Michael and I have had people express a desire that someone would offer a course on how to live in a world of brokenness, hurt, and defeat. Simply, they are asking if daily help is available to face life more effectively. Naturally, as pastors, we share that such a course is available in our sacred Scriptures, the Bible. This collection of thirty-one daily meditations is not a substitute for the Bible. Rather, our intention in these pages is to guide the reader into the vast treasure of God's word, offering guidance where we might look for wisdom for the challenges we are presently facing. The stiffest battle of life is locating the wisdom and strength to stand up to life's difficulties with poise, courage, and strength.

Framed in my home office is a runner's quote: "Something only a runner would understand . . . 'The first mile is a liar. Don't ever trust it.'"[2] Often, life feels like the first mile of a run. We become weary rather quickly. Feelings of despair well up within us, and we sense inevitable defeat. Beaten, we look for someone to come to our rescue. Often, our prayers to God are little more than a request

1. I have read multiple iterations of this wisdom.

2. Source unknown.

for God to deliver us from danger and difficulty. Throughout the Bible, God tells us that the first mile is a liar. We have more inside of us than we realize. God urges us to continue the run. A change of attitude is the most powerful and constructive way we can and must make progress in this life. Then, we hear through the voice of the apostle Paul, "I can endure all these things through the power of the one who gives me strength" (Phil 4:13). God always accompanies us, strengthening us when we are weak and tired, restoring confidence that life has meaning and that we have a purpose. Meditating on these words from Philippians, when that first mile seeks to defeat us, reminds us that we possess an invincible power.

This book is the third volume in a series of books that provide a month of meditations and prayers around a specific subject: the first, *A Month of Prayer: Five-Minute Meditations for a Deeper Experience of Prayer*, and the second book, *A Month of Prayer and Gratitude: Five-Minute Meditations for a Deeper Experience of Gratitude*. As I wrote in each of those volumes, the most helpful practice when using this book is to identify a time of day when you might spend a minimum of ten minutes alone with it and God. Five minutes will be for reading a single meditation along with its prayer of the day, and five minutes will be for stillness, reflecting upon what God may be saying to you through the words you've read. Try praying, "God, what would you have me hear?" and "What would you have me do?" The reader will benefit from reading this book as it is designed: one meditation daily for thirty-one days. Plowing through the book in one or two sittings will only diminish the value of any one of them. *A Month of Comfort and Wisdom* is not so much a book to be read as it is a collection of daily meditations that cultivate, slowly and over time, a deeper experience of God's presence and power that leads to the mastery of life.

Acknowledgments

Emerson once wrote, "I awoke this morning with devout thanksgiving for my friends, the old and the new."[1] As I now enter the last few years of my ministry, I find Emerson's words resonating more deeply than ever before. For nearly thirty-nine years, I have met the demands of ministry with uncommon strength—the strength promised in Scripture that comes from our Lord and the strength of friends who have guided me, encouraged me, and sustained me. The cover of this book bears the names of three of them: Thomas K. Tewell, Michael B. Brown, and Leo S. Thorne. On multiple occasions, I have drawn from the deep well of their wisdom. Consequently, my ministry has been the stronger for them. My life is the richer because of them. Words are inadequate to communicate the "devout thanksgiving" that swells in my chest for the profit that each one of them has brought to the five congregations I have served. It is a considerable honor for my name to appear on the cover of this book along with theirs.

For fourteen years, Nancy Fine, business administrator for the First Presbyterian Church of Delray Beach, has been a valued colleague in my practice of ministry. Her attention to detail, a continuous striving for excellence, and deep love for this church have been an inspiration to my own service to the gospel of Jesus Christ. Michael Brown, Leo Thorne, and I are aware that what we have prepared in this book accomplishes nothing, adds no value to others, unless it is shaped into a manuscript for a publisher.

1. Emerson, *Essential Essays*, 61.

Wipf and Stock Publishers are very exacting in what they expect from a manuscript submission. Naturally, this results in a book of exceptional quality and beauty. Nancy consistently meets those expectations in the preparation of each book I have published with them. Simply, without Nancy, there would be no book.

The Holly House, a ministry of First Presbyterian Church of Delray Beach, serves the women of the church and local community by providing social engagement with one another, regular prayer and support, and unleashing creative talents in art and crafts, producing unique and attractive products that are sold at a holiday bazaar in December. Additionally, they provide a "Step-Above Rummage Sale" each February for the community from donated items from the church membership. Proceeds from both ventures support the capital needs of the church. The church is stronger for these women, both through their efforts to enhance our facility and, more importantly, the sense of purpose and meaning they give to the women of Holly House. This book is dedicated to these women, and their ministry, with gratitude.

Michael, Tom, Leo, and I especially want to acknowledge our spouses, Page Brown, Suzanne Tewell, Dr. Yvonne Martinez Thorne, and Grace Hood, for their own close walk with our Lord and the many ways our ministry is blessed and strengthened by them. The blessings we have received from them are too numerous to count, and our lives are the richer for them. Perhaps the greatest blessing we continually receive from them is their ability to gently remind us of what our most important vocation is.

To you, the reader of this book, we are grateful that you have chosen to be intentional in your walk with our Lord by pursuing the collected wisdom and guidance found in these pages. In the twelfth chapter of Genesis, we are told that God blesses us so that we might be a blessing to others (Gen 12:2, 3). Our hope is that this modest collection of meditations and daily prayers will bless you so that you might be a blessing to others, particularly those who struggle with discouragement and defeat. In 1928, Harry Emerson Fosdick published the article "What Is the Matter with Preaching?" There, he asserts that the endeavor to help people solve their spiritual problems is a sermon's only justifiable aim.[2] Within these pages are not sermons but brief meditations. Yet, it remains our hope that Fosdick would be pleased with the collection before you.

Doug Hood

Pentecost 2025

2. Fosdick, "What Is the Matter," in Graves, *What's the Matter*, 9.

Abbreviations

CEB	Common English Bible
KJV	King James Version Bible
NASB	New American Standard Bible
NIV	New International Version Bible
NKJV	New King James Version Bible

We Laugh to Keep from Crying

(Michael Brown)

"He will fill your mouth with joy, your lips with a victorious shout."
Job 8:21

"Happy are you who weep now, because you will laugh." Luke 6:21b

There's a lovely Presbyterian church not far from where we live that, on Wednesday mornings, has a study group called Laughter and Lamentations. What a great name for a class in this day and age! Some suggest (not just comedians, but psychologists and theologians, too) that sometimes the more we hurt, the more we need to laugh. And, there are always things to laugh about. Humor is not a denial of reality. It is, instead, a gift by which we cope with reality. That theme is beautifully explored in Dr. Susan Sparks's book, *Laugh Your Way to Grace.*[1]

My mom (who from time to time battled depression during her life and who possessed a wild, and sometimes bawdy, sense of humor) often laughed her way to grace. She used to say, "We laugh to keep from crying." The Bible frequently says pretty much the same. Job lost about as much as one can lose: family members, property, land, farm animals, the support of friends, and physical health. But, in the midst of almost indescribable suffering, as the

1. Sparks, *Laugh Your Way to Grace.*

NIV puts it, he was promised that in time God would "fill [his] mouth with laughter, and [his] lips with shouts of joy" (Job 8:21).

In his Sermon on the Plain (Luke's rendition of the Sermon on the Mount), Jesus talked about poverty, sorrow, and grief. But while dealing with those undeniable realities, he added, "Happy are you who weep now, because you will laugh." In the Eastern Orthodox tradition, the word "Easter" literally means "God's laughter." Following the most dire and desperate of all the events in human history, the crucifixion of the Messiah on a Roman cross, Easter came. The stone was rolled away. And according to that ancient liturgical tradition, the heavens were filled with the sound of God's laughter, the boundless joy of knowing that sin and evil and death had no power anymore. We laugh to keep from crying. But even more, ultimately, we laugh because life wins. Love wins. God wins.

Norman Cousins's best-selling book from years ago, *Anatomy of an Illness as Perceived by the Patient*,[2] told of how he went into remission from a serious illness for which there was no known cure. For hours at a time, Cousins would lock himself away and watch films by the Marx Brothers and old episodes of *Candid Camera*. He belly-laughed as he viewed them. Laughter produces endorphins, which, in his case, began to effectively battle the autoimmune disorder that was crippling him. Eventually, doctors were unable to find any trace of the disease whatsoever. Apparently, the Old Testament book of Proverbs was correct when it wrote that "a joyful heart helps healing" (Prov 17:22a). "Blessed are you who weep now, for you will laugh" (Luke 6:21b NIV).

When things are stressful in my life, in addition to practices like prayer and journaling, I often watch videos by comedians like Leanne Morgan, Stephen Wright, and Martin Short as Jiminy Glick, or I turn on the TV and watch old episodes of *Andy Griffith* or new episodes of *Only Murders in the Building*. "We laugh to keep from crying" because, in truth, humor really is good medicine. The Bible even prescribes it when stress or fear has us in its grip. We cannot (and should not) ignore the reality of human pain—our own or that of others. But in the midst of it, or perhaps at the end

2. Cousins, *Anatomy of an Illness*.

of it, the book of Job promises that God will "fill your mouth with laughter, and your lips with shouts of joy" (Job 8:21 NIV). Or, as Jesus put it: "Happy are you who weep now, because you will laugh" (Luke 6:21b). That may be the gift of grace we need sometimes, just to survive.

Blessed God, I am experiencing today a stress-ripened moment in my life, and I can feel myself inclining to the familiar tears. I pray for your strength to open me up to believe in your unconditional and boundless love that my aching heart can be healed. I reach deeply into my soul and thank you for this valuable gift of humor, which has its own ministry. You offer this gift to remind me of my vulnerabilities, my imperfections, my sometimes-wayward ways, and my need for adjustments to my perspective. Humor and its twin laughter can also prompt me to reorient my heart, to step aside and allow a new self to emerge. I will be thankful and smile at the abundant splashes of your beauty on display all around me. It could be that a smile from me today may also offer comfort to someone in need of your grace. Keep me positive today, sweet Jesus. In your wonderful name, I pray. Amen!

Maintaining Calm in the Tumult

(Doug Hood)

"Most important, live together in a manner worthy of Christ's gospel. Do this, whether I come and see you or I'm absent, and hear about you. Do this so that you stand firm, united in one spirit and mind as you struggle together to remain faithful to the gospel. That way, you won't be afraid of anything your enemies do." PHILIPPIANS 1:27–28A

SOME YEARS AGO, A young man shared with me that years earlier, he made a profession of faith in Jesus Christ. However, in the time that followed, he never sought to grow in his relationship with Jesus. Now his life was moving through a crisis, and not moving through it very well. This brought uncommon insight to him. He said, "I never did anything with my faith, so now my faith is not doing anything for me." Apparently, this young man reduced the Christian faith to right beliefs. He confessed before a church that Jesus Christ is his Lord. He believed in Jesus Christ and that was that. Nothing more is required. What he was now learning—in the midst of a personal crisis—is that the Christian faith is not merely right beliefs. The Christian faith is something that we do, and optimally, in a community with others.

In his present tumult, what this man desired is calm. Some years ago, William George Jordan wrote, "Calmness is the rarest quality in human life. It is the poise of a great nature, in harmony with itself and its ideals. It is the moral atmosphere of a life that is self-reliant and self-controlled. Calmness is singleness of purpose, absolute confidence, and conscious power ready to be focused in an instant to meet any crisis."[1] Simply, the person who is calm identifies a singleness of purpose and pursues that purpose with both sturdy confidence and an intentional strength of resolve. This is precisely the point Paul makes in his Letter to the church in Philippi: "Live together in a manner worthy of Christ's gospel" (Phil 1:27). That is our purpose. Further, Paul asks for a steady resolve toward this regardless of external circumstances, whether Paul comes to see them or is absent from them.

A familiar song during the Christmas season suggests that they will be home for Christmas, but as the song develops, that home may only be in their dreams. Nonetheless, there will be joy—whether physically home or home in their dreams. Notice here that joy, or its absence, is dependent on something from outside of the individual—something that is beyond the grasp of the individual to control. Will a loved one be home for Christmas or not? Paul is saying that joy and a life of obedience to Jesus Christ are not dependent upon some external circumstance, not dependent upon whether Paul comes to be with them or is absent from them. Calm is available either way once the mind is focused on a great purpose.

These few sentences of Paul conclude with the promise that fear and uncertainty will not fill the heart if the mind is set upon the single purpose of living for Christ's gospel. If we hand authority to external circumstances for our well-being, we confess our inferiority to them. We grant them the power to dominate us. It is then that worries of every measure stir us to unease, wear upon us, and eventually, we wear down to surrender. Calm dissipates. Paul announces it does not have to come to that. "Live together in a manner worthy of Christ's gospel." Do that, and the natural result is that you will not be afraid of anything your enemies do. Malice and slander, difficulties and hardships, disappointments and failures may assail you. Calmness will remain.

1. Jordan, as cited in Nightingale, *Transformational Living*, 39.

O God of extravagant wonder, I am constantly amazed by the magnificent power you display in the raging of the mighty oceans, and in the gentle breeze which causes me to exhale in awe of you. My life is churning today with boisterous turmoil in and around me. I humbly ask for your grace to release my human struggle into the satisfying inspiration of the Spirit's power. It is my earnest prayer to stay single-minded in being your obedient child and not to allow anything to rob me of the joy I can find in your redeeming love. Yes, Lord, life's unpredictable waves will come, but I will drop my anchor deep in the sweet assurance of your peace and holy calm. In the confidence of your abiding presence, I pray. Amen!

Throwing Away Self-Pity

(Doug Hood)

"Awake, awake, put on your strength, Zion!" Isaiah 52:1a

Captivity for Israel has ended. God has defeated the powers of Babylon and has authorized Israel to depart and head for home to Jerusalem. A new day, with a strong future, now rises for God's people. "Awake, awake!" is God's double imperative to Israel. "Put on your strength, Zion!" The call sounds strangely familiar. "Up and at 'em! Let's get going!" is the more common usage today. These, or similar, words have been uttered by most parents summoning their children awake from their sleep. The image of sleepy children, resisting the call to leave the comfort of a warm bed, is sharp and crisp. The parent can wake the child with a shout and can summon the child from the bed, but it must be the child's own strength that moves them from slumber to a fresh engagement with a new day.

God's present difficulty is that Israel doesn't want to get out of bed. During their captivity in Babylon, Israel had become dulled, inattentive, hopeless, and grief-stricken.[1] Israel had been humiliated by Babylon and had spiraled into such despair and self-pity that it no longer wanted to live. No longer did life offer a driving purpose—only a memory of brighter days. Absent was a radiant hope—only a fading dream. A captivating vision had fled from

1. Brueggemann, *Isaiah*, 136.

their sight. What remained was a history. "Awake, awake!" is God's response to Israel's self-pity. "Put on your strength, Zion!" God was reminding Israel that there was still strength in the people and was here urging them to summon that strength and toss off that negative attitude that had consumed them.

Psychotherapist and author Amy Morin writes that feeling sorry for yourself is self-destructive.[2] Though we all experience pain and sorrow in life, dwelling on your sorrow and misfortune can consume you until it eventually changes your thoughts and behaviors. Morin contends that any of us can choose to take control. "Even when you can't alter your circumstances, you can alter your attitude."[3] This is the clear declaration of God to Israel: the clear call to shake off their indulgence in self-pity, claim the strength that remains in them, and move positively forward toward the future God has prepared for them. God's strength comes alongside our own. It does not do for us what we can do for ourselves.

After Victor Hugo was exiled from his beloved France, he spent eighteen years in the Channel Islands. Hugo once described this exile from the nation he loved as worse than death. Each afternoon, at sunset, Victor Hugo would climb to a cliff overlooking a small harbor and look longingly out over the water toward France. Legend tells us that each day, following his meditations, Hugo would pick up a pebble and throw it into the sea. One day, the children who developed an affection for him asked why he threw a stone in the sea each day. "Not stones, children, not stones. I am throwing my self-pity into the sea." Little wonder that during those eighteen years of struggle, Victor Hugo gave the world his best and most profound work of literature.[4]

Loving Jesus, sometimes the fear I cradle in myself is my most unwelcome enemy. This tiresome task fills me with doubt and self-pity and puts me in a funk. Today is one of those days I am cradling my anxiety, my Lord. I confess it. But I do not want to stay here. I seek to open up my unwilling heart. I want to steal away to hope and

2. Morin, *13 Things*, 20.
3. Morin, *13 Things*, 18.
4. Butts, "*Beware of Self-Pity*," para. 7.

freedom. Compassionate Jesus, give me strength to claim a willing corner of my heart for you. You are with me, as my only true Guide. I take your hand in mine because I cannot make it through this tough moment without you. I can't go alone; I won't. And, God, give me guidance to seek out a human friend for loving support. Help me, my God, in the power of your risen Christ, I pray. Amen.

I Want to See Your Face

(Michael Brown)

"Look, I myself will be with you every day until the end of this present age." Matthew 28:20b

A few years ago, my wife, Page, had surgery. She said to me before the nurses wheeled her out for the operation, "When I wake up in the recovery room, I want to see your face." Were most folks to see my face when coming out of anesthesia, they would think they had arrived in *The Twilight Zone* or were experiencing a *Nightmare on Elm Street*. But (to edit a lyric that Professor Henry Higgins sang about Eliza Doolittle in *My Fair Lady*), I suppose my wife has grown accustomed to my face. Page knows I'm not a surgeon. Therefore, she knew I couldn't fix anything. My presence could not make her well any more quickly than if I had not been there at all. But, she was expressing trust that I love her and would be with her and for her.

"Look, I myself will be with you every day," Jesus said to his disciples at the mount of the ascension, "until the end of this present age." Or, as another translation puts it, "even unto the end of the world" (Matt 28:20b KJV). Or, as we sometimes feel when life is pressing its full weight upon us, "even when it feels like our world is ending." Jesus promised that he loves us enough to be with us and for us.

How many times have you heard someone say, "Looking back, I know I could never have gotten through that on my own"? Maybe you've said that yourself. If we live long enough, most of us understand that sentiment.

A woman I knew many years ago lived alone in a small mill town in mid-North Carolina. Though only in her late forties, she presented as much older. She used a walker, each step slow and halting. She was stooped from the shoulders and neck. Until you got to know her, the woman's speech was somewhat difficult to understand. All that was the result of a near-fatal auto accident years earlier when she was returning from a high school football game with a carload of other cheerleaders. She spent weeks in a major university medical center, hovering between life and death, followed by months in a rehab facility. Despite her circumstances, the woman's outlook on life was surprisingly positive, and she possessed one of the deepest faiths of anyone I have ever known. Her positive perspective, she claimed, was the result of "the kind man who sat in a chair next to my bed every night when I was in the hospital." A nurse? An orderly? A friend or relative from home? The nurses on her floor assured her mother that no one came into her room at night. No one sat silently watching over her. It was a dream, they said. It was clearly her imagination reacting to fear by creating an image of comfort. Years later, the woman said to me, "It was not my imagination. It was my Lord. I saw him, and that gave me the strength to get better. He was there when I needed him, and he always will be."

"When I wake up in the recovery room," my wife said, "I want to see your face." She needed a loving presence to give her courage as she dealt with discomfort and whatever the journey to recovery might be. Sometimes we all look back and confess, "I know I could never have gotten through this crisis or that heartbreak on my own." The good news is that we didn't have to. Jesus promised, and he is unfailingly as good as his word. "I will be with you always, even unto the end of the world" (Matt 28:20b KJV). Or, as my friend put it, "He was there when I needed him, and he always will be."

Faithful God of love, you will never let me go. You see my face with divine clarity, and you also see my broken spirit and wounded heart. Thank you for never ever leaving me on my own. God of surprises, I trusted you back then, and I will trust your healing presence now. Giver of life abundant and sufficient strength, I live in the expectation of your open arms. In the blessed name of Jesus who is with me, I pray. Amen.

Standing Up to Life

(Doug Hood)

"I can endure all these things through the power of the one who gives me strength." Philippians 4:13

Joan Burns, a friend for over eleven years, recently gave me one of the most honest compliments I have received—"What I enjoy best about our friendship is watching you try to be funny!" That comment demonstrates that Joan is the one in our relationship who is genuinely funny. More importantly, the comment demonstrates the strength of our friendship. She doesn't fear damaging our friendship with her candor. That strength of friendship is what we all seek—and need. It is the strength that defines my relationship with my daughter. I will make a silly comment to Rachael, followed by the self-aggrandizement, "I'm so funny!" Rachael's simple response is, "No, you're not!" Naturally, that has become a clever riposte between my daughter and me. Yet, Joan's quip, "What I enjoy best about our friendship is watching you try to be funny," has theological depth: Joan acknowledges, in her humor, that I am actually "trying!"

"I can," begins Paul's remark to the church in Philippi. The emphasis is not on our dependence upon God. We do not expect God to do everything for us—or we shouldn't! There are things that we can do and ought to do. There are things we can endure, though they may not be pleasant. A runner understands this. The first mile is unpleasant for every runner, regardless of physical condition. The first mile is a liar. The first mile will plead with us to stop, that this should be a rest day. Or the lie is that we are not strong enough, or the weather isn't ideal for running. Runners are familiar with the lies of the first mile. So, runners endure the lies and continue into the second mile, where the lies are eventually silenced. Our Christian faith calls forth the same endurance. Our faith does not release us from making the best effort within us. We can face difficulties and obstacles that find their way into our lives. It is simply a decision to stand up to life.

But there is more in Paul's comment to the Philippian church. The "I can" is matched by the strength from God. First comes the resolve that we will stand up to life and make every effort within us to do so. Obstacles, setbacks, and losses will be met with our determination to move through them. That determination will then realize a surge of power that comes from without—the power of the one who gives uncommon strength, the risen Christ. Just as a runner endures the lies of the first mile, the second mile presents new strength for the road ahead. God's strength always comes alongside our effort, the "I can." But our own effort comes first. The first mile must be endured. As we approach the end of that first figurative mile of difficulty, a new spiritual confidence emerges that touches every area of one's manner, disposition, and attitude toward life. The notion of "I can" is not a hope or wishful thinking. It is established upon God's promise of strength.

The stiffest challenge of life is not questioning God's presence when we need God. It isn't asking God to rescue us from difficulty or straighten things out for our family. The stiffest challenge of life is to stop viewing God as a blue genie available to grant our wishes or as a cosmic servant who makes the rough places smooth. God is available to pull us together when we fall into despair and to build upon our own determination to instill courage, strength, and guidance for where we place our next step. God's desire is that we stand up to life with the confidence that we don't stand alone. Every success, every accomplishment, every step into the second mile of our life will be through the power of the one who gives strength. Paul's words here, "I can endure all these things through the power of the one who gives me strength," renew courage when life becomes difficult. Repeated often, these words will become a vital part of surviving that first mile.

O God, help me to stand firm on what I know to be true: that your unfailing presence is always with me; that your grace sufficient is available to support me in all life's challenges that come my way with my name on them; that your Holy Spirit, the most powerful force for good in this world, comes to help me exchange my discomforting yoke for the gentleness of yours; that you see the interior of my heart where no one else sees and loves me unconditionally. I choose to rise and stand confidently today with your help. In the powerful name of Christ, I pray. Amen!

To Those Defeated

(Doug Hood)

"After his deep anguish he will see light, and he will be satisfied."
Isaiah 53:11

These words are spoken by God. They are spoken of someone who has hit a brick wall. Someone who is defeated. Like many of us, there exists a pervasive sense that if they failed once, they most certainly would fail again. They are not alone. It is likely many of us have experienced defeat following a failure—a defeat that whispers in our ear that we are not enough, that the failure is an assessment of our worthiness. Fear takes up residence inside of us and results in a lack of willingness to try something again. Such a position of the heart, a will to surrender when things get hard and avoid at all costs further failure, results in a defeated life. Right here in Isaiah, God promises that the deep anguish of failure may seem like the end, but it is not. When life appears to have reached its end, we are not abandoned. God's will for each of us is that we prosper. "He will see light, and he will be satisfied."

Robert T. Kiyosaki writes, "Failure is part of the process of success. People who avoid failure also avoid success."[1] This is one of the great lessons of history. In science, we think of Thomas Edison, who, following failure after failure, succeeded in inventing the light bulb. In politics, we think of Abraham Lincoln, who

1. Kiyosaki, as cited in Morin, *13 Things*, 180.

met multiple failures and lost election after election before being elected to the United States presidency. Professional sports are replete with stories of athletes who refused to give up, and because of their refusal to be defined by failure, embraced victory. Each one was driven by failure to continually improve, to do better the next time, until success was theirs. They are unconcerned with impressing anyone and do not worry about being perceived as a failure by other people. One person matters, and only one. That is themselves. Failure is not the end but the beginning. The journey may be long, but they refuse to accept anything but success.

Naturally, refusal to accept defeat demands personal responsibility. Deliberate attention to the particulars of any failure provides guidance on what to change, a recalibration of approach, an expansion of methods, and further development of skill. We may not initially understand the reason for our defeats, but we are responsible for the way we carry our defeats. God promises here in Isaiah that we will be satisfied. But we must be a participant; we must play our part. God holds us responsible for cooperating with God's work in our lives. Membership in a gym and securing a personal trainer have no power to transform us physically without our participation. Nor is God a genie that grants our wishes apart from our engagement, our struggle, and our consent to join in God's activity in our lives. Nothing tests us more than our response to failure. The way we take failure is a test of life. It is nothing to fail. It is tragic to surrender to it.

Finally, the promise of satisfaction is much richer than grasping victory, of realizing success in our endeavor. The biblical story of God's engagement with God's people bears witness to the truth that defeat increases the value of life. Moses's forty years in the wilderness were not easy. Moses experienced defeat in his leadership with God's people. Recall the people who chose to worship a golden calf during the long absence of Moses. The people of Israel experienced defeat. Remember the loss of hope in God's future for them and a desire to return to Egypt. Every struggle, every disappointment, every defeat was matched by a fresh encounter of God's grace, God's patience, and God's power. Each developed in Moses and the people a stronger relationship with God. In defeat, values were deepened, a nation was made braver, and a relationship with God was taken to a new level. As Israel entered the promised land, satisfaction was theirs.

Lord God, you are most mighty, most sufficient, most forgiving. You overflow with goodness and with unstinted power and love. I often judge myself too harshly because of my human weaknesses and failures, and these two unkind twins take up unbidden lodging in my heart and mind and prevent me from moving forward. Dear God, open the eyes of my heart to see a new orientation you have ahead for me, to comprehend that there is strength beyond my strength, hope beyond my despair, grace more abundant than my sins, and holy power outstretched to support my weakness. I walk by faith into this blessed assurance awaiting me today. In the strong name of Jesus, my Lord, I pray. Amen!

Unanswered Prayers

(Michael Brown)

"A very strong wind tore through the mountains . . . but the Lord wasn't in the wind. After the wind, there was an earthquake. But the Lord wasn't in the earthquake. After the earthquake, there was a fire. But the Lord wasn't in the fire. After the fire, there was a sound. Thin. Quiet."
1 Kings 19:11b–12

"I've quit praying," the woman told me with more a sense of sadness than defiance. "I've prayed so hard across so many years for so many things, and I can't really see that it's made much of a difference one way or the other. So, I've stopped trying. What's the point?"

From time to time, many of us feel what she expressed. You pray with both faith and urgency, "O God, please . . .," but the prayers seem to bounce off the ceiling. Who hasn't prayed for Russia to stop its assault on Ukraine? For a lasting peace to come to the Middle East? For a cure for some debilitating or terminal illness? For a loved one to be made well? For a marriage to be healed? For a friendship to be restored? But, in the end, the very opposite occurs. And we find ourselves thinking, "I can't really see that prayer made much of a difference one way or the other. What's the point?"

There are, of course, a variety of responses one can make. An old cliche we often hear teaches, "When we pray, sometimes God says 'Yes,' sometimes 'No,' and sometimes 'Wait a while.'" That counsel may well be true, but it's not always comforting when your world is falling apart. Another response, of course, is that God's will is often very different from our own and, therefore, sometimes even prayers passionately prayed do not receive their desired outcome.

Remember when Jesus knelt in the garden of Gethsemane and prayed in agony, "My Father, if it is possible, let this cup pass from me" (Matt 26:39 NASB), but the cup (the cross) did not pass. Often, it is only in retrospect that we finally realize that "No" was the best answer to a prayer we offered, much like Garth Brooks sang in his song "Thank God for Unanswered Prayers."[1] There are moments when receiving something good would, in the long run, prevent us from receiving something far better. All those ideas being stated, it's still difficult when we pray, and, as my friend said, it doesn't seem to make much difference one way or the other.

Perhaps, however, the real difference is not in receiving or failing to receive anything in particular. Perhaps the most powerful aspects of prayer are religious faith and self-understanding. When I pray, I am acknowledging that I believe there is someone near in the midst of the earthquake, wind, and fire, and that someone is both accessible and caring.

Whereas that spiritual certainty may not do or undo anything specific, it does empower me by reminding me that I do not face life alone. God is present, as God was with Elijah when the storms came, to listen and to care. Knowing that, I can forge my way ahead, however steep or difficult the road may be. Likewise, to speak a prayer is to eavesdrop on my own soul. It is to hear the truths, the needs, the fears, or the loves that lie deep within me, too often buried or repressed. I pray, something pours out, and I find myself thinking, "Where did that come from? I can't believe what I just said!" In that moment, I recognized who I actually am.

Does prayer accomplish anything? It reminds me of who and whose I am. And those just may be the most important answers to prayer at all.

1. Garth Brooks, "Unanswered Prayers," on *No Fences*, Capitol Nashville, 1990, compact disc.

Spirit of the living God, hover gently over my often-wandering and all-too-anxious heart in this moment of prayer. Remind me, faithful God, that I need to put greater distance between your divine role in prayer and my expectation of answered and unanswered prayer. My greater need is to end this long winter in my soul and build a deeper and more trust-filled relationship with you, even when my heart is slow to clench this truth. Give me the spiritual wisdom to embrace this plus for my life, help me add this grace-filled illumination to my praying, and grant me the humility to let go and let God be God in my life. This is my prayer today in Jesus's name. Amen.

Tears in a Bottle

(Doug Hood)

"You yourself have kept track of my misery. Put my tears into your bottle—aren't they on your scroll already?" Psalm 56:8

Many of us have a bucket list—a list of experiences we would cherish before death. They require no explanation to others, no defense. They are deeply personal. Further, an explanation may reduce the depth, color, and richness of personal meaning. Most people recognize that what is experienced deeply can rarely be expressed with words. Words are useful for the communication of thought. They are less useful for conveying deeply held emotions, feelings, and convictions. A strong writer can approach this depth of meaning better than most. But always, words have a reducing effect. Permit me to simply state that high on my bucket list are three experiences I would value: a cameo appearance in a stage production of the musical *RENT*, being a balloon handler in the Macy's Thanksgiving Day Parade, and sharing a cappuccino with David Hyde Pierce.

Some will remember that David Hyde Pierce played the character of Niles Crane on the popular television series *Frasier*. On three occasions, I have enjoyed watching David Hyde Pierce on a Broadway stage: *Spamalot*, *Curtains*, and *Vanya and Sonia and Masha and Spike*. If I were to have an occasion to have a private conversation with Pierce over coffee, my first question to him would be, "What makes you cry?" An answer to that question often points to deeply held convictions; it points to those values, struggles, and principles that grip our hearts. Again, words are limiting. But they can point another in the right direction. An answer to the question, "What makes you cry?" provides a window into the depths of another's soul.

Naturally, tears come in a rich variety. A powerful conviction of truth draws tears to my eyes every time. I simply cannot read in Luke's Gospel the story of Simeon taking the infant Jesus in his arms without my chest becoming heavy and tears forming in my eyes. Here, Simeon recognizes this child as God's salvation. This is a story that reaches beyond the descriptive; it is evocative. In faith, Simeon sees God's decisive hand in the unfolding drama of human history. Grief is another variety of tears. Old Testament teacher Walter Brueggemann helps us with understanding this passage from the Psalms. Here is a confidence that God has kept, treasured, and preserved "my tears"; that is, all the pain and suffering that the psalmist has experienced. "God is the great rememberer who treasures pain so that the psalmist is free to move beyond that pain."[1]

There is an ancient Jewish practice that provides care in times of misery and grief. A small bottle is provided to collect the tears of anguish and loss. The top of the bottle has a small hole in it that would allow those tears to evaporate over time. When the bottle is completely dry, the time for grieving is over. The psalmist wants us to know that God has a bottle with our name on it. When tears of grief flow, God collects them in that bottle. This is how seriously God takes our grief—how God honors and shares in our loss. But there is a small hole in the top of that bottle. Over time, the tears will evaporate. When the bottle is dry and our eyes are clear, we see that God remains. And God redirects our eyes to tomorrow.

Lord, I lay bare to you all that I am today, especially my wet tears flowing freely and unchecked in my grief. I hurt, Lord, and this raw pain seems closer than your presence, I sadly confess. The labyrinthian corridors of my not-so-silent struggle may not immediately change, dear God, but, ultimately, they will cost me my fears, my

1. Brueggemann and Bellinger, *Psalms*, 254.

anxieties, and the struggle with my loss. My deep cry is really freeing me to confront an often-neglected spiritual reality that my daily hunger is for you. I exhale in this freedom. I pray this prayer upward in the name of Christ. Amen.

Disillusioned at Christmas

(Doug Hood)

"They asked, 'Where is the newborn king of the Jews? We've seen his star in the east, and we've come to honor him.'" Matthew 2:2

Speed bumps are intentional obstructions along routes traveled by motorized vehicles to slow drivers down. They indicate the need for caution, that something unusual is present and requires particular attention for safe navigation forward. Ignore the speed bump, the driver will experience a jolt and, perhaps, minor damage to their vehicle. Matthew's Gospel has placed a speed bump in the Christmas narrative. If ignored—or not noticed—the reader will miss a greater truth that Matthew wishes to convey. Rather than hurrying to the end of the story, Matthew wants the reader to make a rich discovery as the story unfolds: The magi made much of their journey to Bethlehem without the light of the star.

Notice the speed bump: the magi enter the city of Jerusalem and make inquiry as to where the "newborn king of the Jews" is born. They began their journey to find the baby when they saw a star in the east, but now the light of that star is unseen. Now they must ask for directions. Consulting with the chief priests and legal experts, King Herod learns that the Christ was to be born in Bethlehem. Herod then sends the magi on their way in that direction. Only when they come to Bethlehem do they see the light of the star again. This is why the magi "were filled with joy," Matthew tells us. They were on the right road, and the promise of that star was about to be realized. Finding the child with Mary, his mother, the magi fell to their knees, honored him, and presented their gifts.

Matthew is writing to a particular people who are on the cusp of disillusionment and abandoning their faith. The decision to follow Christ has resulted in estrangement from those family members who don't believe in Jesus. Moreover, followers of Jesus are no longer welcome in Jewish worship. Divided from their loved ones and unwelcome in the faith community, it is easy to question if they are on the right road. The easy path would be to admit a mistake in following Jesus, abandon the Christian movement, and return to the embrace of family and cherished worship. The light that began their faith in Jesus has dimmed considerably, and now they are traveling in the dark.

So it may be with our faith. Oftentimes, we do not experience the power, the light, the vitality of the faith we once experienced. Difficulties overwhelm us, the road becomes dark, and we are disillusioned. The path that was once clear is now an unknown way. Matthew wants us to remain confident in the promise. Circumstances may require that we stop, reassess our route, and seek guidance as the magi did in Jerusalem. There is much in the world—and in our lives—that we cannot change. It's not our task to repair the brokenness all around us. What we can and must do, says Matthew, is to speak of the promise of "the newborn king" that comes in the midst of that brokenness, kneel before him in worship, present our gifts, and trust that it will be enough.

How often, my God, do I get thrown off by life's inconveniences, when things do not go my way, when mystery comes wrapped in an unknown package without name? Did I miss something here, Lord? Are you for real and is this Christian faith worth it? Did you really come to earth as a naked, vulnerable babe in Bethlehem's manager? Blessed God, may Christmas this year remind my often-questioning heart of your blessed invitation to live with partial understanding in the community of your saints everywhere. Emmanuel is with us. God has come, and he is coming again. In the name of the holy child, Jesus, I pray. Amen.

Just Two Things

(Michael Brown)

"'This is his commandment, that we believe in the name of his Son, Jesus Christ, and love each other as he commanded us. Those who keep his commandments dwell in God and God dwells in us, because of the Spirit that he has given us.'" 1 John 3:23–24

A long-time friend (who has been hearing me preach for more than twenty-five years) said to me recently, "You have two sermon themes." I've been at this work for about half a century, so one would think that's a fairly conservative estimate. I answered that by accident, in that much time, a preacher would trip over more themes for the pulpit than just two. But he stood fast with his assessment of my preaching. "Nope," he argued, "your consistent themes are the presence of God and the power of love. Just two themes—and they are enough."

Whereas I don't want to force myself into a theological fraternity that is clearly above my pay grade, those two themes were apparently also closest to the heart of John. How did he put it? We "love each other as he commanded us. Those who keep his commandments dwell in God, and God dwells in them."

The first essential of faith is trust in the presence of God. That is indispensable both for celebrating and surviving the world in which we live. I write this meditation while watching the sun rise over the beautiful Atlantic Ocean. The sky is a rainbow of pinks and purples, softly erasing night's darkness with morning's light. Waves are kissing the shore. Some gulls swoop down in search of breakfast, while others are content simply to sit on the water and bask in the loveliness of it all. An older couple walks the beach, hand in hand, celebrating the nearness of another whose mere touch shelters them from loneliness. A new day has come with color and beauty. "The heavens declare the glory of God, and the firmament shows his handiwork" (Ps 19:1–3 NKJV).

You just can't look at something this majestic without believing, and, also, without learning some valuable faith lessons. The gulls know that there is one who will provide them with food (one who will meet their needs). By the simple touch of another's hand, the aging couple knows that they are not alone. When we get still enough to observe life, great truths break through: among them that one who loves us and will provide for us is present with us. "If I take the wings of the morning, and dwell in the uttermost parts of the sea. . . . Your right hand shall hold me" (Ps 139:9, 10 NKJV). God is present. If we just pay attention, that truth is almost impossible to miss.

The power of love is the second essential of faith. "This is my commandment," Jesus told his disciples in the upper room, "love" (John 15:12a). It really is that simple.

That's why the Bible refers to the power of love more than seven hundred times. It keeps hammering away at the fact that unless we put love into practice in our daily lives, nothing else will ultimately make sense (or bring lasting contentment). We can acquire or achieve, find position or power, obtain fame or fortune, but without a commitment to loving people, Paul said we become merely "clanging gongs or clashing cymbals" (1 Cor 13:1b).

My friend, the late Dr. Arthur Caliandro, used to say that at the final judgment we will be asked one question and only one: "How well did you love?" He based that conviction on the words of Jesus in Matt 25, when our Lord said exactly the same thing. Love may mean standing up and speaking out on an urgent societal issue. It may mean personal involvement with a local charitable agency. It may mean taking the time to listen to one who is lonely or infirm. It may mean the way you speak to people at work or in public places. It may mean what you communicate at home (and how you communicate it). Usually, it involves all the above. But this truth is undeniable: If we fail to love, we fail to discover authentic life.

"Your consistent themes," my friend observed, "are the presence of God and the power of love. Just two themes—and they are enough." In the end, it may be that they are all there is.

All-wise God, there are many matters I struggle with as I make my journey in this world. There are many questions about you, unanswerable, I carry in my heart. Although I may never fully resolve them in my always-questioning spirit, may I never doubt your unconditional and uncompromising love for me, and may I continue to believe in your non-erasable presence in my life. Holy Spirit, I attach my faith to these two nonnegotiables and walk by faith to a treasure far greater than my best-loved possession on this earth. In this quiet moment, I pray that your presence will urge me daily to seek a deeper and more abiding relationship with you. May your love challenge me to incarnate in my lived experiences your love at home, at work, at play, and all around me, including people I have difficulty loving. I confess my deep need for you today, Lord, in Jesus's name. Amen.

Destructive Regrets

(Doug Hood)

"Martha said to Jesus, 'Lord, if you had been here, my brother wouldn't have died." John 11:21

Here is an example of the destructive nature of regret. Martha has lost her brother, Lazarus. Rather than accepting that death is inevitable for each of us, that Lazarus's death was not the result of an unfortunate accident or tragedy, Martha begins to question what could have been done—what might have been executed differently that would have prevented this loss. Martha has engaged in the most common form of grief, the "If only . . ." cycle of questioning that impedes healing. We are familiar with this form of grief: "If only you had been here, my brother wouldn't have died." "If only I had arranged things differently." "If only I had made a different choice, taken another turn." We recognize Martha's sentiment as our own. It is a response that flows from unnecessary and harmful personal responsibility.

This appearance of grief is usually born on the morning after a loss or crisis. And it sometimes continues until we draw our final breath, holding us in an unwarranted prison of self-blame. It is a sorrow that drains away vital strength, a grief that consumes our lives. The crippling result is the loss of an inward peace and the capacity to meaningfully live for others. Others who love us, who look to us for encouragement, strength, and direction, are deprived of our friendship. We are simply crushed under needless regret. "If only I had called the doctor earlier." "If only I had noticed the signs, had paid more attention." One devastating loss now precipitates another. We may still have breath in our lungs, but no longer do we bring value to our homes, our communities, or to our network of relationships.

Suppose for a moment that there was something we could have done. Suppose that we could have made a different choice or might have taken another course of action. What then? The question that presses from this passage of Scripture is: Who is our God? Martha identifies Jesus as "Lord." What does the lordship of Jesus mean for us? Martha's profession of faith, of her belief in Jesus's capacity as Lord, startles. It is a faith in a lord who has limited ability. She confesses—though unintentionally—a belief that Jesus's redemptive power is only available while Lazarus remained alive: "Lord, if you had been here, my brother wouldn't have died." But her brother has died. Hope in anything more is abandoned. Nothing more can be done, apparently, even by Jesus. Jesus didn't arrive in time.

The Bible tells us that Jesus wept at the tomb of Lazarus. There has been considerable conjecture as to why Jesus wept. The Bible remains silent on this question. Some have suggested that Jesus simply gave expression to the natural human response to the loss of a dear friend. Others have offered the suggestion that Lazarus's death provided an entrance into paradise, to everlasting life with God, and now, Jesus was about to take that away by bringing Lazarus back to life. Each of these suggestions completely ignores what Jesus heard from the lips of Martha: "if you had been here." Jesus heard an incomplete faith: "if only." The very gospel of Jesus's power is that things that are broken are repaired. If, unintentionally, we have gone astray, Jesus is the one who makes the crooked straight and gives life where the world only sees death.

Merciful God, I have holy work to do, and here I sit with a stout case of self-orientation. My world has become selfishly personal, and I am embracing the discomforting coziness of my pain. I am closing off myself from the beautiful tapestry of your children, from the amazing splendor of your creation, from your insistent call to love my neighbor as I love myself, and from the blessing of allowing your radiant light seeking to shine through me. Merciful God, your Christ offers me by his glorious resurrection a new light by which to see. He whispers into my dull ear and into the brokenness of my grieving heart the challenge to accept loss as a normal part of living in this world. I surrender my heart today to the joy of being other-oriented with compassionate living that makes me more Christlike. In the strong name of Christ, I make this prayer. Amen.

Victory on Our Knees

(Doug Hood)

"I live on high, in holiness, and also with the crushed and the lowly, reviving the spirit of the lowly, reviving the heart of those who have been crushed." ISAIAH 57:15

RECENTLY, GRACE AND I spent a weekend in the Florida Keys with two dear friends. In addition to sharing meals together, shopping, stimulating conversation about our families, and an evening of bicycling, the four of us summoned the courage to try something we had never done before—paddleboarding. The popularity of the sport seems to be growing exponentially in South Florida, particularly the Keys. It looked fun and appeared to be a sport that would be easy for beginners. It was not. Paddleboarding challenges both core strength and balance, and beginners spend more time falling from the board than standing. My wife, Grace, was perhaps an exception; other people asked me how long she had been paddleboarding.

After several attempts at standing—and failing—Grace said to me to begin on my knees: "You have more control on your knees." Hearing my wife's words, my friend commented, "I hear a sermon in there somewhere!" Naturally, I was frustrated that I was unable to master paddleboarding immediately. But then, where would have been the satisfaction in that? Satisfaction with life is often preceded by considerable effort and discipline. So it is with our Christian faith. We must experience failure on our own before we can value God's presence and strength that enables us to stand. The pinnacle of joy and satisfaction in our faith is our communion with the risen Christ. That communion begins on our knees in prayer—our demonstration that we can't do life apart from God.

To be a Christian is to follow Jesus. And his own life was no leap from the cradle in Bethlehem to the victory of Easter morning. Victory implies that something was defeated. Between birth and resurrection, Jesus lived deeply. It was a life that knew suffering, betrayal, and abandonment. We experience with Jesus the victory and joy of the resurrection because we know all too well his hell of loneliness and pain. It was a hell that Jesus defeated because he spent so much of his life on his knees. Grace is absolutely right: "You have more control on your knees."

The central question that confronts many today is: Where is God in the darkness of the present world—the darkness that seems to defeat a hope for tomorrow? Isaiah declares that our God lives with the crushed and the lowly. God is not only present in our darkness; God is at work, "reviving the spirit of the lowly, reviving the heart of those who have been crushed." God did so for Jesus. God will do so for us. What is needed is that we wait for God's victory on our knees.

God of infinite mercy, sometimes I approach life with a strident, can-do attitude. "I can do this" often gushes from my confident lips. Slow me down, Lord, and help me to understand who gets the glory in this way of living and to shy away from the illusion of self-sufficiency. Be ever-present in my heart today, Lord, and show me the awesome delight of working together with you in all things, large and small. Open my eyes, Lord, to see that you are accomplishing your holy work in the secret crevices of my pain and suffering and in the darkness of this unkind world. As I bow my knees today in deep trust, help me to comprehend that you have wisdom beyond my wisdom and power available to help me release my vain boasting. In the name of Christ, I pray. Amen.

Not Why, But What and Who

(Michael Brown)

"But I know that my redeemer is alive, and afterward he'll rise upon the dust . . . whom I'll see myself—my eyes see, and not a stranger's."
Job 19:25, 27

A course I teach every semester at High Point University is entitled Biblical Themes. It's designed to explore the great themes of our Judeo-Christian faith: law, grace, sin, salvation, the centrality of love, the search for meaning, incarnation, spirit, etc. One of the lectures is always about *theodicy* (a theological consideration of the reality of suffering in a world governed by a good God). Rabbi Harold Kushner wrote a book about that entitled *Why Do Bad Things Happen to Good People?*[1] It became a bestseller because the book's title is a question almost everyone asks if they live long enough.

Our classroom session on theodicy is always based on the Old Testament book of Job, a study in human suffering vis-à-vis the existence of a loving God. Job lost everything a person can imagine losing, except for his belief in God's presence. He was grief-stricken, angry, confused, unsure why he had done his best in life and seemingly had been repaid with nothing but hurt and heartache. And yet, even when a loved one told him to "curse God and die" (Job 2:9), he did not give up his belief in the divine. Mind

1. Kushner, *When Bad Things Happen.*

you, he did feel that life was unfair. He did feel the covenant had not been honored, even though he had kept his end of it. He didn't just glibly say, "It is what it is." Job kept crying out, "Why?" Suffering made no sense to him, as often it makes no sense to us. But amid questions for which he could find no answers, Job never let go of one fundamental belief: "I know that my redeemer is alive."

When at last Job got his moment to pose his question to God about why he had suffered so seriously after having done his best, God answered, "Where were you when I laid the earth's foundations?" (Job 38:4a). It was not a curt or unkind response. Instead, it was God's way of replying that even if the reason for suffering were explained to Job, no mere mortal could wrap his mind around it. Furthermore (and even more importantly), getting an answer to "Why?" wouldn't change a single thing. If you could determine why an illness or accident took the life of a loved one, that knowledge wouldn't bring the loved one back. It wouldn't change anything. So, God helped Job understand that the important questions are not "Why?" but instead "What?" and "Who?" What do I do to survive? To move forward? What resources do I have at my disposal? What friends provide shoulders I can lean on? What inner strengths do I need to call to the surface? And, who is God? Do I make God into the enemy who caused the pain, or the ally who will help me survive and overcome it? Knowing why something happens doesn't undo it. But knowing what steps to take and who is the God that promises to walk with you on the journey helps one to survive it.

Simply appealing to reason and faith provides the insights we need for the journey. Reason confesses that we cannot effectively live life in epochs or seasons. Nor do we heal from major hurts overnight. Faith partly offers the simple recognition that we don't make life's journey alone. Life is lived in moments, not seasons. You don't have to heal in a day or a month or by any imposed calendar or guideline. Just inch your way forward, one day at a time, one step at a time. And trust that even when you don't understand, still the one who loves you is walking with you—day by day and step by step. "I know that my redeemer lives, and that in the end he will stand on the earth. . . . I myself will see him with my own eyes" (Job 19:25, 27 NIV).

All-knowing God, who ever told me that I will be happy and have everything I want to be fulfilled in this life? You know that my heart is all too susceptible to this misguided kind of thinking I have for myself, my family, my friends, and my loved pet, too. Holy God, open my spirit a little wider to confess and believe today that you alone have all the answers for this life in all the contours of its mysterious ways. I don't. My deeper need, dear God, is to have a more robust and intentional relationship with you in all the syllables of passing time. In my human frailty, I pray for the inner strength and faith I need to lean more closely into your abiding presence and wisdom. I seek your guidance today and every day. Thank you, my God and living Redeemer. Amen.

Plants of Steel

(Doug Hood)

"I can endure all these things through the power of the one who gives me strength." Philippians 4:13

The garden center of Home Depot features a selection of plants ideal for home or office called "Plants of Steel." They are plants that seem to thrive in apparent adversity. Where other plants would wilt for lack of water and sunshine, these plants enjoy optimal vitality from neglect. I have purchased several of these plants, and it is fascinating to watch them flourish in spite of—or because of—my inattention to their care. They seem to have a preference for hardship.

These plants offer encouragement for spiritual life. Difficult circumstances, though never sought, can provide growth. Such growth is clear in the lived experience of the apostle Paul. In this letter to the church of Philippi, Paul is in captivity in Rome. His supreme mission of preaching the gospel of Christ appears to be at an end. No longer does Paul have the stimulus of travel, the joy of enriching itineraries, or the delight of preaching the good news over the broad landscape of Asia and Greece. That open road has been narrowed to the walls of a prison cell. Yet, there is an absence of gloom in Paul's writing. Throughout this letter of Philippians, there is present incomparable strength and beauty.

Paul's imprisonment does not usher in a season of gloom. Rather, what Paul experiences is a time of spiritual graces. He writes of losing everything for Christ, only to realize that what he lost has no value compared to what he has gained in a relationship with Jesus. Within prison walls, Paul realizes the broad range and wealth of his spiritual inheritance. While some of his friends referred to his misery, Paul writes of his joy. Though some regretted his poverty, Paul boasts of possessing all that he needs. What appears to be a season of winter for Paul is transformed into an opportunity to be clothed in a fleece robe of strength and hopefulness.

Some today become very poor in difficulty and adversity. When in the natural rhythm of life, they reach desert places or what may feel like an endless winter of the soul; they live without any cheer. Sourness and fretfulness encompass them as the prison walls surrounded Paul. All of life becomes a menagerie of unpleasant things. Worse, they feel left alone. Paul's incredible witness is that this doesn't have to be their story. Paul writes letters from prison not to share his misery with a sympathetic ear. He writes to invest in others. Investments in other people, in the ministry of our Lord, scatter the gloom, brighten the place of our dwelling, and preserve the leaf of our soul from withering. We become plants of steel! Moreover, we will know such joy that the desert of the soul shall rejoice and blossom like a rose.

O God, the prison house of my own making seems to be closing in on me. My fears and anxieties enclose me like prison bars, steeling my cheerless and captive heart. Holy Spirit, brood over the chaos in my depleted soul today as you did in the beginning of creation's dawn. I open my heart and soul to be free again and to fly with abandon into your joyous light and unfailing love. Blessed God, remind me that to live like Christ is an invitation to serve others, even with all my scars and vulnerabilities. In the name of Jesus, I pray. Amen.

Disillusionment with God

(Doug Hood)

"The burning sand will become a pool, and the thirsty ground, fountains of water." Isaiah 35:7

There is, perhaps, no greater disappointment in life than to experience disappointment with God. Missed opportunities, unrealized dreams, and friends who fail us are no small matter. They can be debilitating at times. Yet, most people also recognize that such disappointments are the stuff of life. With a strong network of family and friends, many find that they are able to push through such disappointments. But what are we to do with our disappointment with God? This is the most shattering of disappointments. "No longer is there a wide, comfortable margin between peace and the edge of doom," writes that great Scottish preacher James S. Stewart.[1] Disillusionment with God is startling, surprising, and overwhelming. In a deep spiritual sense, such disillusionment is taking up residence in the desert.

Isaiah has a word for those desert moments—or days. In dramatic fashion, Isaiah speaks of a grand reversal: "The burning sand will become a pool, and the thirsty ground, fountains of water." With incredible verve, he takes the most frightening and cynical judgment of the world that says that this life is nothing more than "burning sand" and reverses it. God is not absent, nor will God

1. Stewart, *Wind of the Spirit*, 70.

remain silent. The word from the Lord is that the desert places of life will become an oasis, living water that quenches our fears and dispels the darkness.

What does this mean? In effect, Isaiah acknowledges his common experience with ours that life is full of disappointments, broken dreams, and dashed hopes. Moreover, Isaiah is no stranger to fears that come like a bolt of lightning, unnerving our sense of comfort and security. But he also wants to remind us of history: Israel's history of a God that is never far off, a God that appears in the midst of struggle and uncertainty with the hand of a shepherd, confidently leading us forward into God's future for us. In every situation, even when the darkness of the hour seems to have the upper hand, grace reigns.

Understand, of course, that the very struggle with disillusionment dispels any notion that faith is always experienced without struggle. Any spiritual journey occasionally moves through desert places, where the ground is hot and parched. But, Isaiah asks that we steadily move forward, particularly when our steps are labored and weak, for a wonderful discovery lies ahead of us, the same discovery that Isaiah made. Present circumstances that seem like burning sand will, by God's promises, become a pool of cool water. Additionally, you will find yourself in the company of those who have discovered that they would rather travel the most difficult road with God than any other road without him.

Holy God, disappointment with you is a spiritual matter. It may be, and help me here, Lord, that I too often want my own way and my human answers, not yours. This struggle is real in my soul today. Disrupt my contrary thinking, merciful Lord, and this stubborn weakness in me. I desire to hear deep in my troubled soul your voice of calm calling my name. Give me the spiritual ears to hear and the bold courage to answer, "Here I am, Lord. Here I am." In the abiding strength of Christ, I pray. Amen.

The Intersection of Loss and Hope

(Michael Brown)

"Jesus said to her, 'I am the resurrection and the life. Whoever believes in me will live, even though they die.'" John 11:25

If you live long enough, you will lose someone or something you love: a person, a home, a marriage or romance, a job, a pet. Even moving from one place to another involves the loss of a community of friends and a sense of belonging. So, what can we do when grief has us in its grip? Among other things, we can practice the fine (and healing) art of remembering.

(1) Things We Know *From* Those We Remember

The New Testament book of Hebrews states: "We have such a great cloud of witnesses surrounding us" (Heb 12:1b). They are there—the ones who taught us our most valuable life lessons. They remain around us and within us as long as the lessons we learned from them are remembered and applied. Your mom's devotion to church, your dad's commitment to family, your professor's insistence on academic (and personal) integrity, your friend's loyalty, your neighbor's positive outlook—all those influences made (and continue to make) you what you are. The donors may no longer be present, but the impact they left behind lives on. And, thus, in a very real sense, they live on, too. "We have such a great cloud of witnesses surrounding us" (Heb 12:1 NASB).

(2) Things We Know *For* Those We Remember

The Gospel of John tells of a promise Jesus made to Martha and Mary following the death of Lazarus (their brother). He said, "I am the resurrection and the life. Whoever believes in me will live, even though they die" (John 11:25). Only one chapter later, Christ made a promise to all his disciples. The NIV phrases it this way: "And I, when I am lifted up from the earth, will draw all people to myself" (John 12:32). Jesus assured believers that his resurrection would not be a solitary journey but, rather, that he would take his friends with him. That's what we know for those we have loved and lost. Beyond this life is another life where death shall be no more.

A clergy friend told me of a woman in his church who lost her husband and her son-in-law in an automobile accident. Her world was torn out from beneath her, leaving her understandably devastated. In time, however, as my friend put it, "she came back to life." Psychologists call that "new normal" (the time when you have processed pain sufficiently to move forward again). He said she told him that the key for her was some words written by a friend who sent a sympathy note. The words simply said: "What feels like the end for you is a new beginning of unbroken joy for them." "My love for them was stronger than my sadness for myself," she told my friend. "I learned to embrace their new lives of unbroken joy."

"We have such a great cloud of witnesses surrounding us" (Heb 12:1 NASB). As long as we remember the love and lessons received from those who went before, they will live on in and through us.

"Whoever believes in me will live, even though they die." Those whom we have loved and lost are not really lost at all. Instead, when Jesus made his journey home, he took them with him to new lives of unbroken joy.

Dear God, show me in my loss that I am not on a lonely, deserted island isolated with my most familiar friends: me, myself, and I. Your precious word reminds me of the great cloud of witnesses, exemplars of this faith I cherish. I also live today with faithful and gifted Christlike influencers around me. We are all making this temporary journey with hope to arrive at our permanent abode with you, but not yet. Come to think of it, Lord, may my life today be your instrument to help someone get ready for their eternal home with you. In the awesome power of our resurrected Christ, I make this prayer. Amen.

When God Seems Distant

(Doug Hood)

"I'm convinced that nothing can separate us from God's love in Christ Jesus our Lord." Romans 8:38a

Tommy Lasorda, former manager of the Los Angeles Dodgers, tells about an experience he had in church. One Sunday, he was in Cincinnati for a ball game against the Reds. That morning, he went to early morning Mass and happened to see the Reds manager there. They were old friends and sat beside each other during Mass. Afterward, the Reds manager said, "Tommy, I'll see you at the ballpark. I'm going to hang around a little." Lasorda said that when he reached the door, he glanced back over his shoulder. He noticed that his friend was praying at the altar and lighting a candle. He said, "I thought about that for a few moments. Then, since we needed a win very badly, I doubled back and blew out his candle."[1] Though misguided, what a powerful demonstration of faith in God's presence and activity!

Countless people today long for that deep confidence in God's presence and activity in their lives. God seems distant to them. They plod through each day, fearful, anxious, and burdened with uncertainty. Some may remember once having a close relationship with God, but that was a long time ago. Prayers seem to never rise higher than the ceiling—and that is when we even

1. Bouknight, *Authoritative Word*, 30.

feel like praying! The good news is that this is not an uncommon experience in the Christian faith. Just as people can grow apart in relationships with one another, so we can drift away from God. As Thomas Tewell once said to me, the difference is that in human relationships, both parties contribute to the distance. But, in a relationship with God, the reality is that we drift away from God. God never drifts away from us.

In those moments when God seems distant, what are we to do? Perhaps an experience I had this past week will help. My daughter, Rachael, is in Norway—a studio photographer for the Holland America Cruise Lines. It's not uncommon for Rachael to work twelve- and fourteen-hour days. Wi-Fi is limited, and with her long hours, it is difficult to "connect" with her by telephone or by other means in real time. Just this week, Rachael reached out to me via Facebook Messenger. She said that for a limited time, she was available to receive a phone call from me and that she really would like me to call. Immediately, I moved something that was already on my calendar to another time and placed the call. Do you see what happened? Suddenly, my greatest desire was to speak with my daughter. To do so, I had to make the time.

We reconnect with God the same way. We move beyond our desire to be close to God and carve out time from our busy lives to simply be still in God's presence. We open the Bible and read expectantly, asking God to speak powerfully through the words that we read on the page. We learn from our reading more about God, about God's good desires for us, and we learn what God requires of us. We spend time together with God. And we listen: we listen deeply in the silence following our reading to the hunches, the promptings, and the direction we sense from God. As we respond positively, the distance we once felt from God begins to close.

Faithful God, I pray for strength to close the gap between us. I confess that I am the guilty party here. My anxieties and fears and lackluster commitment to you enticed my weak heart to stray. My spiritual battery needs to be recharged, Lord, so I invite you into my neglected prayer station. Remind me that I need to pay attention to Jesus, my Lord, every day of my life and that I can rely upon your unfailing presence, 24/7. Wrap your warm cloak of unfailing love around my cold heart. I need your warmth again. I miss the blessing and friendship of the tender relationship we share in those quiet moments. Sweet Holy Spirit, keep me coming back, again and again, to experience your constant and wise activity in my life and in this troubled world. Amen.

Unbeatable

(Doug Hood)

"I was beaten with rods three times. I was stoned once. I was shipwrecked three times. I spent a day and a night on the open sea. I've been on many journeys. I faced dangers from rivers, robbers, my people, and Gentiles. I faced dangers in the city, in the desert, on the sea, and from false brothers and sisters. I faced these dangers with hard work and heavy labor, many sleepless nights, hunger and thirst, often without food, and in the cold without enough clothes." 2 Corinthians 11:25–27

Sometimes it appears that the apostle Paul had a hidden charm that both protected him from discouragement and defeat while providing navigation for his ministry. With every possible force at work against him—every possible obstacle to moving forward—Paul was simply unbeatable. His journey seemed impossibly long, and there were lengthy stretches during which he had to endure much hardship and loneliness. What's more, Paul kept a careful journal of each difficulty encountered, every challenge he faced, and the deprivation he endured. His purpose for recording each was simply to force the question—can anyone survive experiences such as these, one upon another, by their own strength, their own resources?

Paul's answer is, "No." Every difficulty, challenge, and deprivation presented an opportunity for Paul to proclaim available strength that was not Paul's—the strength of the risen and active work of Jesus Christ. Storms are part of the normal climate, and adversity is part of normal life. Paul utterly rejects the false notion that a formula is at work that shields us from the strong winds and turbulence of day-to-day life. Rather, Paul's desire is to point to his own life and demonstrate a steadying hand that holds us and strengthens us in the storms. Life is full of annoying and costly interruptions and opposing forces that are bent on defeating us. Paul urges that we make the winds of opposition occasions for relying upon God.

That legendary football coach of Notre Dame, Knute Rockne, once summoned his players before a game and said, "The team that won't be beat, can't be beat."[1] Rockne was not here proclaiming the strength of Jesus for his players. He was appealing to the uncommon courage, strength, and persistence that lie within each of us. Many of us engage in the game of life without our best effort, settling for something just below our actual capacity. Tremendous effort to overcome life's difficulties is rare; people often accept defeat easily, naming what is possible as impossible. These are not the challenges Paul speaks of. Paul lifts his eyes to something higher still, to what is impossible were it not for God's strength.

Paul continues this discussion that if it's necessary to brag, he will brag about his weakness that people may observe that he is insufficient without Jesus—that people may see the wondrous work of Jesus through him. There are doors that we cannot walk through and storms we cannot endure on our own. That is when we make every difficulty an opportunity to lean into Christ and draw from Christ's strength. The strength that sustained Paul through every force that sought to stop his ministry is available to every one of us. In our hearts, we may ask, "Can I endure?" Paul gives the answer: "In Jesus, we are unbeatable."

Gracious God, many people who have crossed my path have displayed the indomitable spirit of endurance because of their faithful confidence in Jesus Christ, our risen Lord. Is there something big or small that I can learn from them? Or, my Lord, I can recall when in the past you rescued me and gave me your grace to move forward.

1. Frank, "Persistence Is the Key," para. 16.

And I did! Alleluia! Inspire me to unleash my courage today, I pray, to pull myself up with the help of your Holy Spirit and bravely welcome the path I travel with you. Keep your persistent voice in my ear and help me fully rely on your dependable power. I make this prayer in the powerful name of Christ. Amen.

A Quiet Place

(Michael Brown)

"When Jesus heard about John, he withdrew in a boat to a deserted place by himself." Matthew 14:13

An out-of-state tourist in Florida was fishing in a marshy inlet when his small boat capsized. Hanging on to the side of it, the man feared there would be alligators in the inlet and his life would be at risk. He cried out to an old fisherman on the shore, "Help me! Please! The alligators will attack me." The old guy didn't even look up. He just called back, "There ain't no gators in this inlet. There used to be, but they're all gone now." With that, the fisherman relaxed. The sun and water were warm. He decided to enjoy it and did a slow, lazy backstroke toward land. Growing curious, once more he shouted to the man on the shore and asked, "What did you do to get rid of the alligators?" Again, without looking up, the old man answered, "We didn't do anything. The sharks ate 'em."

Daily life, with its rapid pace, incessant demands, strains, and stresses, sometimes makes us feel like we're surrounded by sharks. Financial crises. Relational estrangements. Health concerns. Social pressures. Guilt. Grief. Loneliness. The expectations of others that seem impossible to fulfill. There is no magic wand to wave that can make it all disappear. So, how do we cope with our pressure-laden reality? How do we survive the sharks in our waters?

When the stresses of the moment and the needs of the masses bore down upon Jesus, Scripture says, "He withdrew . . . to a deserted [solitary or quiet] place." He didn't run away from life, but he did retreat long enough to "restore his soul"(Ps 23:3 NKJV). He understood that in order to continue pushing forward with strength and effectiveness, sometimes temporarily, we have to pull back just to breathe.

Norman Vincent Peale used to tell a story about his close friend Desi Arnaz. Both as a performer and, especially, as head of Desilu Productions, Arnaz's responsibilities were mammoth. He told Dr. Peale that one way he coped with that was to slip away from time to time to a small house on the Pacific Coast. He would take off his watch as soon as he entered and not put it back on till he left. While there, he ate when he was hungry and slept when he was tired. Otherwise, he would bathe himself in solitude and silence, watch sunrises and sunsets, and give his mind a chance to rest. He said he always returned home with renewed energy and deepened creativity. "He withdrew . . . to a quiet place." We all need that. For you, it may be reading, quilting, biking, hiking, gardening, golfing, swimming, fishing, museums, movies, or a host of other things that restore your soul. You cannot outswim the sharks if you are weary. You cannot be of significant help to anyone else if you are exhausted. That's the reason the Ten Commandments include the instruction to set aside personal time for sabbath (rest). "He withdrew . . . to a quiet place." If Jesus needed it, so do we. Take care of yourself. It's the only way there will be enough of you left to take good care of anyone or anything else.

O God, I take time now to name the challenges swimming around in my tempest-tossed waters today. I pause and relax my soul. As I surrender to you in this moment, my prayer is not for you to fix the many vexing challenges in my life. I inhale deeply and turn inward and relax my anxious spirit. Slow me down, Lord. I need time for self-care and to be in your holy presence. I pray for holy renewal. I submit to you my misguided desire and my idle aspirations to do it on my own. I seek heavenly strength and wisdom to let go and let God, and I ask you to check the rising tide of my fears and my tendency to doubt your precious love for me. I praise you for the rest and calm you will give me today. In the name of the Prince of Peace, I pray. Amen.

Living Positively with Our Handicaps

(Doug Hood)

"So I'll gladly spend my time bragging about my weaknesses so that Christ's power can rest on me." 2 Corinthians 12:9b

Bragging about our weaknesses is uncommon. What is customary—even encouraged—is that we "hide" our weaknesses and present the illusion of a life that is lived in a tranquil manner that is deep and even and unhindered by frailties. One unfortunate result is the deep disillusionment that is experienced when we find our heroes far too human, with frailties and weaknesses like our own. We look for people who seem to have no limitations, no handicaps, and no imperfections, and we aspire to be like them. In no small manner, people with weaknesses are not considered worthy of our admiration and praise.

Naturally, the danger of finding such a person, a person who is unencumbered by difficulties and imperfections, is to know someone who also possesses considerable conceit. They need no one; they require nothing for their journey through life, not even God. Worse, when understood correctly, their perfection fails to inspire those of us who struggle with handicaps. Another's perfection can only result in our despair. This is why Paul "brags" about his weaknesses—Paul's interest is that we praise only God and that we find in his broken, imperfect life reason for encouragement as we struggle with our own handicaps.

Paul did pray multiple times that his handicap might be removed. That is a demonstration of his humanity. It is an honest prayer that we have no doubt prayed ourselves. Yet, our spiritual condition is developed, positively or negatively, from the place of our weaknesses. For many, the first and instinctive reaction toward our limitations is a negative attitude—a rebellion or self-pity. We revolt against our limitations. Such a negative struggle often advances to cursing God. What we fail to see is that disappointment with our imperfection arises from conceit—we expect to be perfect. That is a poor spiritual condition indeed!

Paul's positive and hopeful response to his weaknesses demonstrates that anyone, regardless of their limitations, can make a spiritual contribution to the world. History is replete with stories of people who rise up and make great contributions in spite of handicaps. These are the stories that inspire each of us to push through whatever difficulties hinder us and advance our lives and the lives of others. Anyone fortunate enough to have the charm and looks of a prince, excellent physical and mental health, and be untroubled by limitations fails to inspire those who struggle daily under limitations. It is not easy to estimate the spiritual stimulus that comes into human life from handicapped people who have found that Christ's power is sufficient for them.

O God, my naked frailties stare me stoutly in the face every day and remind me that I am all too human, like everyone else, without exception. In this moment of penitent prayer, blessed Redeemer, I acknowledge my brokenness and my weakness, and I recognize that I live in a fallen world, which can with subtlety seduce me to seek its transient dreams. Blessed Jesus, I believe that you came into this world as a tiny, vulnerable baby dependent on human parents. You became like us, without sin, to demonstrate God's power in your resurrection, to give us confidence to trust God's power in us, to claim our personal resurrection every day, to live as your redeemed child, and to live fully alive, warts and all. Yours is the better way. I walk confidently in gratitude today knowing that your available strength is my sufficiency, my call to action. Amen.

How to Be Miserable

(Doug Hood)

"Love is patient, love is kind, it isn't jealous, it doesn't brag, it isn't arrogant, it isn't rude, it doesn't seek its own advantage, it isn't irritable, it doesn't keep a record of complaints, it isn't happy with injustice, but it is happy with the truth. Love puts up with all things, trusts in all things, hopes for all things, endures all things." 1 Corinthians 13:4–7

The other day, I came across a theme written by Earl Nightingale that he titled "How to Be Miserable." He provided remarkable clarity about some of the things I have been wrestling with recently, clarity about self-inflicted misery. Nightingale writes, "The first step to real, professional-type, solid, unremitting misery is to get all wrapped up in yourself and your problems—real or imagined. Become a kind of island, surrounded on every side by yourself. By turning all of your thoughts inward upon yourself, naturally, you cannot spend much or any time thinking about others and other things. And so, finally, the outside world—the real world—will disappear into a kind of Hitchcock-type fog."[1]

Nightingale continues with a stinging observation that the type of person who chooses misery, who turns inward upon himself or herself, doesn't have much in the wisdom department.[2] Otherwise, they simply wouldn't do it. In the absence of wisdom,

1. Nightingale, *Your Success Starts Here*, 104.
2 Nightingale, *Your Success Starts Here*, 105.

they turn inward and discover that there is not much there. There is a kind of vacuum, and they have to embellish perceived, or real, hurts and slights from others or invent things entirely. Negative—and harmful—behavior is then directed outward toward those who have caused them harm. This behavior may simply be for punishment, to cause pain equal to what they are experiencing, or to manipulate others to meet some relational expectation.

Where Nightingale provides an unpleasant portrait of a miserable person, the apostle Paul provides divine knowledge—or wisdom—for fleeing from misery: love others, particularly when that love is difficult. Paul beautifully expresses the very nature of love by its positive attributes—"love is patient, love is kind." Paul provides additional wisdom by sharing what love isn't and doesn't do—"it isn't jealous, it doesn't brag, it isn't arrogant, it isn't rude, it doesn't seek its own advantage, it isn't irritable, it doesn't keep a record of complaints." What Paul provides is a different portrait from Nightingale, a portrait of a person who actively participates in the unity and well-being of relationships with others.

It is widely embraced that the Christian faith is less to do with the right beliefs and more to do with the right behavior. A person may have a grasp of the Holy Scriptures that is unparalleled, be able to articulate a particular theological position with uncommon clarity, and yet remain untouched by God's transforming power—the transformation that deepens love for God and love for others. Such a faith is a lazy faith because it requires no effort. Love requires effort. Love demands that we struggle against an impulse to turn inward and compile a record of complaints against another. Such love "puts up with all things, trusts in all things, hopes for all things, endures all things." It is a love that knows no misery.

My faithful God, fact-check: You alone are God, the compassionate, unconditional lover of my soul. Help me to see without distraction today that I am surrounded by your love above me, beneath me, on right and on my left, in front of me, and behind me. Your love is the same for everyone else in this world. In the quietness of this private moment of prayer, I surrender to the prompting of the Holy Spirit in my heart: to help me make my prayer more than words;

to summon the personal anointing I need to be more loving of my neighbor; to lay to rest the stridency of cold dogma so that I can share your love with others; to plant seeds, not of discord, but seeds of unity and peace and harmony; to decide to be understanding and not be judgmental. I will choose to be kind and gracious today, Lord, because God is love, because I am loved, and because God challenges me to love in return. With all my heart, I want to be intentional about being obedient to you and your love. In the power of Christ's servant-exampled love, I pray. Amen.

Where Could I Go?

(Michael Brown)

"'Come to me, all you who are struggling hard and carrying heavy loads, and I will give you rest.'" Matthew 11:28

A phrase all of us have heard throughout the years is the question, "Where could I go but to the Lord?" Those words offer a prescription for peace in a world where peace is sometimes seriously difficult to find. And on those occasions when we do find it, it's rarely because of anything external or anything we managed to accomplish on our own. In fact, it defies rational explanation. Paul called it a peace that "exceeds all understanding" (Phil 4:7).

Robert Duvall is almost universally acclaimed as one of the greatest actors in movie history. To me, for all his outstanding body of work, he was never better than in his fascinating movie *The Apostle*. The close of that movie finds him dressed in the striped prison uniform of days gone by, doing hard labor in a field under a hot summer sun, smiling and quoting words of faith and praise.[1] The circumstances of his life were demoralizing, but his inner spirit refused to be defeated by outer circumstances. He possessed a peace that exceeded rational understanding. Just a movie? No. Instead, it is the testimony of centuries of faithful people who survived hardships and heartaches not because they were necessarily strong, but rather because they knew someone

1. Duvall, dir., *Apostle* (October Films, 1997).

who was . . . Someone they could lean on when otherwise they would fall . . . Someone who invited them to "Come unto me, all you who are struggling hard and carrying heavy loads, and I will give you rest."

As I write this meditation, I have no idea who will read it. But I do know that whoever reads it will be carrying some heavy load in his or her life. They will be bearing up under some burden, perhaps unseen by any human eye. If you are that person, then hang on to this promise. There is someone who sees and who knows and cares about what you are going through. He clearly stated that he does not desire for you to bear your burden alone. There is a source of strength beyond our strength, a source of hope beyond our means to make lemonade out of lemons. He is leaning forward now to hear the prayer you whisper. And he is saying, "Come unto me, all you who are struggling hard and carrying heavy loads, and I will give you rest." Just say the word, and his hand will take your own, providing peace that exceeds understanding.

Holy God, search me in all the nooks and crannies of my aching heart by your Holy Spirit. I welcome your grace-dripping invitation today to receive your promised inner peace. My prayer today in my struggle is to move from my usual cohort of almost vain words to decisive action. With your blessing and strength, I will arise and release this load I have been carrying for way too long. I lay down my struggle at your feet. Receive it, gentle Jesus. Receive me. Thank you, Lord God. Amen.

When the Door Remains Closed

(Doug Hood)

"Meanwhile, Peter remained outside, knocking at the gate."
Acts 12:16a

Here is a story for everyone: a story of someone who tried and failed, but refused to give up. Peter was one of Jesus's disciples. At a critical hour, he failed Jesus by denying him three times. But Jesus never failed Peter. Following Jesus's resurrection, his continued embrace and love for Peter launched Peter into a preaching ministry of considerable zeal and devotion. Up and down the countryside, Peter gave witness to the power of the risen Christ to change lives. Peter's primary exhibit for his testimony was his own life. Soon he found himself enmeshed by hostile forces and, finally, preached himself into prison.

Prayers were made for Peter by the Christian communities that he started and were now growing as a result of his preaching. One night, an angel came to Peter, placed the prison guard into a deep sleep, released the chains from Peter's hands, and opened the prison doors. An important detail of this miracle story is that the angel instructed Peter to put on his sandals. The angel was able to place the guard into a slumber, release Peter's hands from the chains that held him, and open the prison doors. Yet, the angel holds Peter responsible for putting on his own shoes. Apparent in this small detail is that God will always do what we cannot do, but

God will not do for us what we can do. Peter was capable of placing his shoes on his feet.

Peter, now freed from prison, goes out into the dark, hiding in the thickness of the night from Roman soldiers, and makes his way to a home where he hoped to be received and cared for. When Peter knocked at the outer gate, a female servant went to answer. Recognizing Peter, and overcome with surprise and joy, the servant runs back into the house with the grand announcement of Peter's release. Yet, in her amazement and delight, she forgets to open the gate and let Peter into the residence. "Meanwhile, Peter remained outside, knocking at the gate."

Peter does not shrug his shoulders and walk back into the night, commenting, "It's no use." Peter continues to knock. Peter is resilient. He will not give in or give up. Through his persistence, Peter reveals the grandeur of his trust in God's continuing presence and care. Many of us will stand—at some moment in our life—before a closed door. The closed door may be a job opportunity that never materializes, a romantic relationship that is never found, or an illness that lingers—health seemly more and more elusive. Before that closed door, life asks, "Will you continue to trust God in the face of bitterness and disappointment?" Peter stands before a closed door, unafraid, determined to see it through. His strength is located in God's fidelity, demonstrated in his past. That same strength is available to us when we stand before a door that is closed.

Dear God, this rusty, old door before me seems shut tight, closed, impossible to open. Is this door closed because of the almost-forgotten past pain I caused my friend; because of something I am refusing to let go; because of that bad habit I am giving power to take me captive every time; because of that pill of strident unforgiveness I take every day; because of that stout tendency to believe I can make it on my own without you; because of that paralyzing indecision of not knowing when to act or when to wait? Blessed, Lord, I trust your love and grace, and in your faithful mercy I seek your light. Knock, knock, knock, in the name of Jesus, my Christ, I pray. Amen.

Brokenness at Christmas

(Doug Hood)

"Then Mary said to the angel, 'How will this happen since I haven't had sexual relations with a man?'" Luke 1:34

While I was in college, I studied for a semester in Coventry, England. My dormitory room was in Kennedy House, located on the campus of Coventry Cathedral. The clergy of the Cathedral were my faculty. Each Friday, at noon, I was required to participate in a brief service of worship in the ruins of the original Cathedral destroyed during the Second World War. Imagine that experience of worship with me. I gathered with a small number of people in the chancel area of the Cathedral, and the charred walls of the Cathedral embraced our worship. Brokenness was magnified by the destruction from a world at war. Yet, amid the visible brokenness, a pastor would take bread, give thanks to God, break the bread, and share that this bread was the bread of life for us. It was a remarkable contrast—visible brokenness to the eyes with a spoken promise of life.

Something like that is how the Christmas story began. There is an unanticipated pregnancy—"I haven't had sexual relations with a man." Then, as now, such a pregnancy shattered the respectability of the woman. Mary is poor but struggling to live by the rules of a respectable society. Then, the unexpected. An angel appears to Mary, and the message from the angel alarms her. There is a pregnancy, and now nothing makes sense. "How will this happen?" asked Mary. Life is already difficult for Mary. But now, due to no fault of Mary, everything has become worse. In that day, a woman found pregnant outside of marriage could be stoned to death. Loss of respectability is one thing. But the prospect of stoning now multiplied the brokenness, except for one thing. Within the brokenness, there is the promise of life, not simply the life of an unborn child, but a child that would bring life to all people.

At this time of the year, people often ask the wrong questions of the Bible. The predominant question at Christmas is the implausibility of a pregnancy without a sexual relationship. Naturally, this is a scientific difficulty. Pregnancy always follows predictable rules. And right here in this teaching from Luke's Gospel, the predictable rules are not at play. Yet, there really is nothing in this story that asks us to reduce it to scientific inquiry. That is the wrong question. According to this teaching, the right question is not a scientific one but, rather, a personal one. Mary is surprised. Surprised by an unexpected visit from an angel. Surprised to learn that she was about to receive something she was not anticipating. It is this element of surprise that is essential to reading this Christmas story correctly. God has intruded on Mary's life.

No one welcomes brokenness. Life is disrupted, often with considerable woundedness. We may go to church to seek escape, to receive a word of inspiration, or to find a community that will embrace and love us. Yet, like that worship in the old Coventry Cathedral, brokenness remains, surrounding us on every side. We wring our hands about the conditions that have fallen on us. Perhaps we even ask, as Mary, why this has happened. We didn't plan on any of this. But, if we are honest, neither did we plan on the serendipitous surprises of life that delighted us, nor the friendships that have nurtured and strengthened us. The Christmas message of Mary's visit from the angel is that God is present amid the brokenness. We need only to pay attention. What we thought would be our ruin may be a new beginning filled with new life and possibilities.

Dear God, your Emmanuel of Christmas is not only God with us, but also God for us. Your presence has come, holy God, not to protect me from the brokenness of this world, but to remind me that life will bring disturbances and disruptions and uncertainty. Keep showing me, God of infinite wisdom, that "God with us" does not imply that we will get all we want, that we will have all the answers we seek, that we will cultivate gardens of beautiful flowers without those prickly thorns. "God with us" also includes a red-stained cross, dear God. We each live with the irony of singing "merry Christmas" while bearing our own personal cross and nails. God with us and God for us offers us in our lonely stable the bright star of hope, and joy, and peace, and love abiding deep in the heart. In the name of the Christ, God's Eternal Light who came to us, I pray. Amen!

The Grace of Listening

(Michael Brown)

"Don't you have eyes? Why can't you see? Don't you have ears? Why can't you hear?" Mark 8:18

People hear but fail to listen. At least, that's what the Bible teaches. So says Isaiah (6:10), Jeremiah (5:21), Ezekiel (12:2), and Jesus, who in the Gospel of Mark asked the poignant questions: "Don't you have ears? Why can't you hear?"

I heard a man say some time ago, "The world consists of so much jabbering. So, I've learned to retreat into my own headspace where it bounces off me. I hear the noise, but I'm really selective about when I choose to listen." I get it. But, what if some of the jabbering (noise) is actually a cry for help? A cry to be noticed? To be seen? To be, for a precious and sacred moment, a little less alone?

My childhood pastor, the late Dr. Harlan Creech, used to talk about "the ministry of being there." He contended that we rarely possess the power to resolve many (perhaps most) of the pains and problems we observe friends enduring. We have no magic wand to wave that can make all their suffering or sadness disappear. But what we do have is presence. We can be there with people. For people. And at the heart of healing presence is the act of intentional listening. Tuning in. Taking someone's words seriously. Because when we take what another person says seriously, we communicate that we take them seriously. It's part of the ministry of being there, the grace of listening.

When my children were small, if we were seated on the couch with the TV on, and if one of them was trying to tell Daddy something but receiving no indication that I was listening, my children would physically take my face in their hands and turn it toward them. "Look at me," they were saying. "Listen to me. I need you more than you need that television program." "Don't you have ears?" Jesus asked. In our politically fractured society, where we spend so much time shouting at each other, how much stronger could our nation be if we who are polarized would simply listen to one another with respect and a desire to understand? In our homes, how much more connected might we feel if we set aside disciplined time every day simply to listen to one another? How much stronger could our prayer lives become if part of praying for us was to be silent and still, saying to God, "Speak, Lord. Thy servant heareth" (1 Sam 3:9 KJV)? How much deeper could our friendships grow if we learned the beauty of the phrases "Tell me about it" or "I'd like to hear more about that"? And, in a culture where 75 percent of adults claim to feel a certain measure of loneliness, couldn't the shadows give way to light for at least some of them if you and I would practice the grace of listening? Who is taking your face in their hands even now, crying out to be heard?

As followers of the one who took all people seriously, failing to listen to others (and, thus, failing to take them seriously) is failing to follow him closely enough.

Blessed God, I pray that you will nudge me to look away from the distractions that come to dull my spiritual ear. I want to remain alert today to the gift of the deep listening I could gift to someone. Teach my often-distracted heart to discern the sound of loving silence, and to embrace the wisdom I need to listen to the voice of another. I desire to give this gift to my spouse and partner, my children and grandchildren, my colleagues, my neighbors, and my friends. Merciful Savior, I add to this list my enemies and those who don't like or love me. And, Lord, keep teaching me to be still and to listen for that still, small voice of your Spirit, who seeks to be my faithful Guide to everyone I meet today. In Jesus's name. Amen.

Fruitful Disappointments

(Doug Hood)

"I'll visit you when I go to Spain. I hope to see you while I'm passing through. And I hope you will send me on my way there, after I have first been reenergized by some time in your company." Romans 15:24

I once knew a woman whose romance had gone on the rocks. She made a grand announcement to her work colleagues that she was never going to permit herself to fall in love again. "You only get hurt," she said. I was a young graduate student struggling in the romance department myself, so I remained silent. Fortunately, an older and wiser woman who was our supervisor made the observation, "If you deal with each disappointment that way, you don't live." I don't recall how many work associates were present at that moment, but each of us became silent as those few words sank deep into our hearts. The supervisor continued, "Reassess that relationship. Take something useful from it. Make it fruitful for the next."

The apostle Paul wanted to go to Spain. He had his heart set on it. Paul's zeal for preaching the gospel of Jesus Christ compelled him to reach the outermost rim of the world. What Paul got was a prison cell in Rome. Like my work colleague, Paul was disappointed. Life's unexpected turns and twists never permitted Paul to take that journey to Spain. That one historical fact dispels the notion that those who follow Christ are never disappointed and never experience disruptions in their own life journey. Paul wanted Spain. Paul got a prison cell. How Paul responded is instructive for us. Paul used that time in prison to reassess God's claim upon him, and Paul wrestled something useful from his disappointment. Imprisonment provided quiet time to penetrate deeply into the mysteries of Christ.

Psychologists tell us that suicide, addictions, and some forms of nervous breakdowns are evidence that people are ill-equipped to manage disappointment. Loss and disappointment, regardless of the magnitude, deprive us of our ability to think and act beyond ourselves. Our focus on disappointment becomes so sharp that we are unable to see what remains positive in our lives. Consequently, loss and disappointment shrink our life to the exact size of our desire that is unmet. Popular speaker and author John Maxwell encourages us along a different path—encourages us to embrace failure and disappointments, extracting from them lessons that result in us "failing forward." It is then that those mistakes, failures, and disappointments become stepping stones to something so much more.

Few people have the opportunity to live life on the basis of their first choice—whether that be a choice in career, a spouse that "checks all the boxes," or some other longing. Paul wanted to go to Spain. He got a prison cell. A large majority of us will find that life moves in directions that are not of our choosing. That is precisely when the Christian faith tells us that we should get something out of every experience, every new direction, even out of disappointment. The bulk of the New Testament is letters written by Paul—many of them written while in prison! After twenty-some years as an itinerant preacher, Paul gets a prison cell. At last, Paul found the quiet time to think deeply about what he had learned of Jesus Christ and pour those thoughts out in a written form. That would be Paul's greatest contribution to the Christian church.

Dear Lord, help me to respond fully to life's unpredictable ways that come to teach me the way of your redemption. May my spirit bend to the work of Christ in me, even in those experiences that seem disappointing. I have insufficient evidence to know where life will lead, but sufficient faith to believe in your goodness. Stir my spirit, dear God, to surrender to your wise leading as I challenge myself to give you my anger, my frustrations, and my vulnerabilities. Enlarge the borders of my interior life today. I seek fresh power from you to help me incarnate your love to this distracted world. I trust your benediction on my future. I make this prayer in the name of Jesus. Amen.

The Allure of a Defeated Life

(Doug Hood)

"I was given a thorn in my body." 2 Corinthians 12:7

Few things are as unfortunate as seeing a woman or man losing heart and all sense of hope, drifting into apathy, and finally despair. When a sense of defeat is permitted to take residence in life, frustration and inaction are too frequently the results. The face becomes sullen, the head is held low, and the shoulders sag. Bitterness grows, the result of an erroneous belief that life has dealt a raw deal or that others have received better opportunities. Left unchecked, the self-pity sentences them to low levels of achievement. A strange comfort is found in simply giving up, experiencing a certain allure of being defeated.

History is replete with men and women who have experienced hardship, anguished over setbacks, and struggled with handicaps—physical, mental, and emotional. Any one of them may have been resentful and rebellious—and many have—with bad behavior the consequence. Yet, there are others who rise above the circumstances of their lives, press forward with unbelievable determination, and consecrate their lives to the service of others. The apostle Paul stands among them. Paul moved through life hindered by "a thorn in the body," but produced nearly two-thirds of our New Testament.

Rather than giving up and accepting defeat, Paul labored under his handicap. Naturally, Paul—like any of us—preferred that the handicap be corrected, the difficulty removed. On three occasions, Paul asked the Lord for this. But the handicap remained; the thorn wasn't removed. But Paul's prayers were answered. "My grace is enough for you," answered God (2 Cor 12:9). With God's answer, Paul committed himself to do the very best he could do with what he had. His life and ministry were a vessel of hope for everyone he encountered. To his children, Theodore Roosevelt continually cultivated a hopeful disposition—and in doing so, charged the atmosphere of his home with hope.[1]

Paul sought to demonstrate in his life that there is no limitation, no misfortune, no burden of sorrow, suffering, or loss that the human spirit cannot rise above. He endured much of each. But Paul went deeper than self-discipline and self-determination. Paul triumphed over it all because he sought God. Perhaps this was the finest message that Paul left the church—that when the allure of defeat tempts the heart, Paul calls us to that deeper place where our life is open to the grace and power of Almighty God.

Dear God, open my eyes to see the clues your spirit is giving me to rise above this weight I am carrying. Perplexed and questioning I am, and I cannot see clearly. It is difficult for me to express at this moment the anguished, obedient prayer of your Son, "Thy will be done." Most merciful God, inflame the dullness of this almost-willing spirit and downcast heart, kindle with your Spirit's spark the lackluster courage in me, and stir the embers of faint hope hidden in my broken heart. Uphold me by your powerful strength today and help me rise above my weakness into the joy and freedom you are offering. Your answer may not come today, Lord, but I will keep trusting. Amen.

1. Summerfield, "*Like Father, like Son*," 7.

The Comfort of Communion

(Michael Brown)

"While they were eating, Jesus took bread, blessed it, broke it, and gave it to the disciples, and said, 'Take and eat. This is my body.' He took a cup, gave thanks, and gave it to them, saying, 'Drink from this, all of you. This is my blood of the covenant, which is poured out for many, so that their sins may be forgiven.'" Matthew 26:26–28

The Gospels tell us that on the night he was betrayed, Jesus had dinner with his closest friends (who were like family to him). He spent time surrounded by them, sharing bread and wine with them, offering ministry to and receiving strength from them. And just a bit later, he took a handful of them with him to the garden of Gethsemane. They couldn't change what was about to happen. But, their presence kept him from having to face it alone. Jesus both offered and experienced comfort at the holy table *and* through what we call "the communion of the saints."

Many years ago, I served a church near Charlotte, North Carolina, that, rather than gathering on Christmas Eve, always observed Christmas night communion. They thought the last act of Christmas should not be unwrapping presents, eating turkey, and watching football. Instead, it should be gathering as a family of faith at the Lord's Table to say "Thank you" for the true Gift of the season. It was not a large church. They had a small staff. There were no associate pastors.

One particular year, while I was serving there, my mother was buried on Christmas Eve. But, there was no one else to lead the service and serve the sacrament on Christmas night. So, I was present—broken, wounded, empty, going through the motions, but present. I had a four-year-old child at home who didn't understand the sadness in our house at Christmas that year. My father was with us, having lost his wife of almost half a century. That night, I seriously struggled just to be there, let alone to provide anything of meaning for those who came to worship.

When the first group of congregants who had received the bread and wine stood, they didn't return from the altar to their pews. Instead, the person at the end of the altar walked over to where I stood and hugged me. The next person did the same. And the next and the next until they had all held their minister close in a gesture of sympathy and love. The following group, who knelt for communion, did the same thing before returning to their seats.

Eventually, every single individual who came forward to receive the sacrament that night hugged me before returning to their pews, many whose faces were wet with tears. For all the books I had read about theology, and for all the courses I had taken in seminary, I think that was the night when I learned what "the communion of the saints" actually means.

In church, we receive the comfort of Christ's promise: "This is my blood of the covenant, which is poured out for many, so that their [our] sins may be forgiven." And, when tough times come, we also receive comfort from the communion of the saints, those who hold us close and hold us up so that we may survive the darkness.

Dear God, open my spiritual eyes to find someone in need of love today. Help me reach out to someone silently praying in their personal garden of Gethsemane: someone needing extreme comfort and healing; someone craving human touch; someone experiencing the darkness of loss and grief; someone beckoning me to lift my eyes higher, further, deeper than my personal pain. Merciful God, can I trust your blessed sacrifice to help me pray for and be an instrument today to bring spiritual courage to a co-sufferer? I can, with your help, Lord, for not one of us should face darkness alone. In the name of Jesus, I pray. Amen!

Letting Go of Anger

(Doug Hood)

"Let go of anger and leave rage behind! Don't get upset—it will only lead to evil." Psalm 37:8

"No man can think clearly when his fists are clenched," writes George Jean Nathan.[1] We need to reach no further than personal experience to accept the truth of those words. Anger destabilizes and diminishes our capacity to make sound judgments. Chances are strong that many of the worst choices you've ever made occurred in moments of anger. Family disagreements result in family estrangement. Differences in political ideology result in poorly spoken words that magnify simple differences into vitriol, even cruelty toward another. Bad behavior flows from hearts that we once never imagined had such capacity. Anger becomes a palatable emotion that gathers strength unto itself as a tropical storm organizes into the destructive force of a hurricane. The teacher of the Psalms is correct—anger that isn't released in a healthy manner leads to evil.

Here in Ps 37, the people of God are angry. The source of the anger is people experiencing success though they do not honor God and do not follow the way of the Lord. It is a spiritual predicament that is very present today. When keeping the faith

1. Nathan, as cited in Goulston and Goldberg, *Get Out of Your Own Way*, 25.

becomes difficult and honoring God requires a level of discipline, restraint, and personal sacrifice, others ignore God and advance, even prosper, in all their endeavors. Fairness seems absent. The result is a stumbling into frustration and destructive anger. We are bewildered by the incongruence of the equation of life: the faithful struggle and the faithless thrive. Mark Twain's words are instructive: "Anger is an acid that can do more harm to the vessel in which it is stored than to anything on which it is poured."[2] What is unfortunate, argues Travis Bradberry, is that this knowledge is rarely enough to help people keep their anger in check.[3]

The teacher in this psalm is asking God's people to place their frustration and anger into God's hands. After all, God's hands have been shown again and again to be really good hands. These are the hands that separated the sea for Israel to pass through when they were pursued by the armies of Egypt. These are the hands that fed Israel for forty years in the wilderness. These are the hands that continue to direct the people in the way of faith and obedience. Our hands are insufficient, certainly not sufficient for such a range of volatile emotions. Such provocation results in a mood that is unpleasant, uncertain, and destructive. The teacher knows that. So, the teacher urges that we do not allow anger to overtake us, but to wait for what the Lord will finally do. Here is a lesson that Israel will learn again and again.

Psalm 37 invites the people of God to another way. It is finally the way of trust in God. Then, we are persuaded to hold to this other way—to clench this other way rather than to clench anger. Certainly, there will be moments when we will seek to take back into our own hands the anger stirred by injustice and hatred in this broken world. These will be moments when we fool ourselves into believing we would be better stewards of what is just and right than God. God's hands are even large enough for such foolishness. And they are patient hands, waiting for us to discover again that such anger in our hands becomes an irritant to our own sense of well-being. It is then that the great teacher asks us once again to

2. Twain, as cited in Bradberry, *Emotional Intelligence Habits*, 157.

3. Bradberry, *Emotional Intelligence Habits*, 157.

hand the anger back to God. Once we are clear that this is where it belongs, we become less worrisome and more expectant of the wonder that God will reveal.

Merciful God of unlimited compassion, I struggle today with my weaknesses. I bring my anger to you and place it on your altar of forgiveness. My soul is being drained by the diminishing power of anger. As I enter this private place of prayer, I come to where you are, and you come to where I am. May the radiance of your love and mercy cleanse and soften my open heart to accept your forgiveness and to release my anger to you. Free me to walk confidently with your strength, and may my heart overflow with gladsome music today as I commune with you. Make me a force for good and grow in me your kindness, mercy, and love. In the compassionate name of Jesus, I pray. Amen!

Not Waiting for Happiness

(Doug Hood)

"I'm not saying this because I need anything, for I have learned how to be content in any circumstance. I know the experience of being in need and of having more than enough; I have learned the secret to being content in any and every circumstance, whether full or hungry or whether having plenty or being poor. I can endure all these things through the power of the one who gives me strength." PHILIPPIANS 4:11–13

HAVE YOU NOTICED HOW many people have delayed their happiness? They seem to believe that if they can achieve a little more success, acquire a little more wealth, or marry the right person, then they will possess happiness. Happiness, they believe, is what follows effort, time, and, perhaps, a little luck. It is as though happiness is somewhere out in front of everyone who is industrious enough to pursue it. Happiness is something to grasp, they believe, and their minds remain fixed upon it until they have taken ownership of it. Striving day upon day toward the possession of happiness, what they miss is that the secret of happiness is already present in the lives of those who long for it.

Paul's letter to the Philippian church provides the secret of happiness—as God's people, we are to live in humility, looking out for others more than for ourselves. That is a great reversal of the commonly accepted formula for happiness. Essentially, Paul teaches that if we are always chasing after happiness, happiness always remains beyond our grasp. On the other hand, if we occupy ourselves with looking out for others, adding value to other people, and promoting their welfare, happiness quietly joins God's people and takes up residence in them. Paul is urging God's people to break free of the tiny little world of themselves and join the great enterprise of God's work in the world.

Here, in the fourth chapter of Paul's letter to the Philippian church, Paul further develops the secret to happiness. Having shared the secret of happiness, disclosed in the activity of Jesus who accepted humility to become like us for the purposes of restoring us to God, Paul points to a mysterious strength that converges in our service to one another. That strength comes not from any person or from the community of God's people, but from the outside. It is God's strength. There is far more going on when God's people join with one another for the promotion of the welfare of others. The same Christ who became human to serve now empowers and enables God's people in their service to one another.

Shortly following the death of his wife, J. R. Carmichael entered a nursing home. Yet, if you inquired about him, you learned that he was never in his room. It seems that each morning, Mr. Carmichael would shower, dress, eat breakfast, and then move from one residential room to another. In each room, Mr. Carmichael spoke with the resident about their family, read the Bible to them, prayed with them, and told them that he loved them. Then it was off to the next room to do the same thing. Mr. Carmichael missed his wife every day, but he never waited for happiness. Happiness found him, as he loved others deeply.

Merciful God, pour out the riches of your wisdom into my heart today that my eyes will truly see, my ears will keenly hear, and my heart will be deeply touched to embrace your way to happiness. Redirect my thinking, Lord, and take me away from my vaporous attempts of seeking to find happiness in all the wrong places. Remind me, blessed God, to embrace the more noble focus that happiness comes from doing, from serving others in the manner of Jesus, our Christ. Give me the love and courage I need to cultivate and share this blessed way of life with everyone I meet today. In the name of Jesus, my example, I pray. Amen.

Taking the Next Step

(Michael Brown)

"Then Moses stretched out his hand over the sea. . . . The waters were split into two. The Israelites walked into the sea on dry ground."
Exodus 14:21a, 22a

On the Sunday following the school shooting at Sandy Hook (where twenty children and six teachers were murdered), our nation was thrown into a deep sense of corporate grief, shock, anger, and fear. I invited three friends to join me in speaking to our congregation at Marble Collegiate Church that morning. One was Rabbi Peter Rubenstein from the famous Central Synagogue on Lexington Avenue in New York City. Peter is a wise man of deep faith. I recall that Sunday how he looked at our congregation and said, "There are times when no answers can help, when no wisdom is enough to explain what happened or why. When we are frightened, travelers standing before the Red Sea with armed tormentors behind us. On those occasions," he said, "all we can do is take the next step when the waters part."

"All we can do is take the next step . . ." Moments come in our personal journeys when the world bears down upon us, and we feel inadequate to overcome or, perhaps, even to cope. You lose a loved one. Your business fails. Your marriage or romance is on the rocks. A friend betrays you. A child walks away, and you are plunged into the brokenheartedness of estrangement. A cherished dream dies.

A diagnosis is alarming. An unexpected financial crisis appears. The list is long. On those occasions, all of us would love to have a magic wand to wave that could make all the bad things better. But there is no such thing. "Better" comes at the end of a journey, not a moment of magic. None of us can make the pilgrimage from pain to healing all in one quantum leap. As Moses directed the Hebrew people to do, and as Rabbi Rubenstein said to my congregation in Manhattan, sometimes the best thing we can do is simply to take the next step.

Maybe that step is to be still and reflect on the status of things. What has occurred? Why does it bring such deep hurt? What can you learn from it? What one thing can you do today to inch your way in the direction of resolution? Or, maybe the next step is simply to confess your humanness. You don't have to be Superman or Wonder Woman. There is no rule that says you aren't allowed to hurt or weep, or that doing so is a sign of inadequate faith. Jesus wept outside Lazarus's tomb. If even he surrendered to a moment of inner pain, you should feel no guilt when your times of fragility come. Or, maybe the next step is prayer, throwing yourself into the open arms of one who is big enough and strong enough to carry you through life's occasional storms.

"Come to me, all you who are struggling hard and carrying heavy loads, and I will give you rest" (Matt 11:28). It could be that the wisest decision of all is simply to trust that promise, to cry out, "Lord, I'm not sure I have the strength to stand at this moment, so I am going to lean on you."

The New Testament word for Holy Spirit is *Paraclete*. It means "one who walks alongside." When the waters before us seem deep and overwhelming, we do not have to conquer them in a single moment of heroic faith or courage. Sometimes all we can do is to take the next step, knowing that the one who loves us and will uphold us is walking alongside.

Blessed God, life stings at the moment, and a daunting sense of darkness invites me to be a stranger in my own skin. I feel helpless. I know not what to say, how to feel, what to think, or believe. I struggle to name this moment of my human brokenness. Ah, ever-present

Lord and friend, I pray for tiny seeds of strength to push me out beyond this earthly experience, to lift up my aching heart and heavy feet, and to take the next step into your open arms. I see you, though not clearly, but I will trust your promise of comfort and abiding presence. I look with the eyes of faith beyond this dark moment to face another day with you. I seek your power, Holy Spirit, as I pray in the powerful name of Jesus, my Christ. Amen!

Bibliography

Bouknight, William R. *The Authoritative Word: Preaching Truth in a Skeptical Age*. Nashville: Abingdon, 2001.

Bradberry, Travis. *Emotional Intelligence Habits: Change Your Habits, Change Your Life*. San Diego: TalentSmart EQ, 2023.

Brooks, Garth. "Unanswered Prayers." By Pat Alger, Larry Bastian, and Garth Brooks. Recorded late 1989. On *No Fences*. Capitol Nashville, 1990. Compact disc.

Brueggemann, Walter. *Isaiah 40–66*. Louisville: Westminster John Knox, 1988.

Brueggemann, Walter, and William H. Bellinger Jr. *Psalms*. New Cambridge Bible Commentary. New York: Cambridge University Press, 2018.

Butts, Thomas Lane. "*Beware of Self-Pity*." https://day1.org/articles/5d9b820ef71918cdf2002858/view.

Chambers, Oswald. *My Utmost for His Highest*. Uhrichsville: Barbour, 1963.

Cousins, Norman. *Anatomy of an Illness: As Perceived by the Patient*. New York: Norton, 1979.

Duvall, Robert, dir. *The Apostle*. October Films, 1997.

Emerson, Ralph Waldo. *Essential Essays*. New York: Warbler, 2023.

Frank, Madeline. "Persistence Is the Key." Ezine Articles, August 23, 2021. https://ezine-articles.com/?Persistence-Is-the-Key&cid=10503510.

Goulston, Mark, and Philip Goldberg. *Get Out of Your Own Way: Practical Lessons for Conquering Procrastination, Fear, Envy, Neediness, Guilt, and More*. New York: Tarcher, 1996.

Fosdick, Harry Emerson. "What Is the Matter with Preaching?" In *What's the Matter with Preaching Today?*, edited by Mike Graves, 7–9. Louisville: Westminster John Knox, 2004.

Kushner, Harold S. *When Bad Things Happen to Good People*. New York: Anchor, 2004.

Morin, Amy. *13 Things Mentally Strong People Don't Do*. New York: HarperCollins, 2014.

Nightingale, Earl. *Transformational Living: Positivity, Mindset, and Persistence*. Shippensburg: Sound Wisdom, 2019.

———. *Your Success Starts Here: Purpose and Personal Initiative*. Shippensburg: Sound Wisdom, 2019.

Sparks, Susan. *Laugh Your Way to Grace: Reclaiming the Spiritual Power of Humor*. Woodstock, VT: Skylight Paths, 2010.

Summerfield, Elizabeth. "*Like Father, like Son: Modelling Masculinity for the Ethical Leadership of President Theodore Roosevelt*." Journal of Values-Based Leadership: Vol. 12: Iss. 2, Article 16. https://scholar.valpo.edu/jvlb/vol12/iss2/16.

Stewart, James S. *The Wind of the Spirit*. Nashville: Abingdon, 1968.

www.ingramcontent.com/pod-product-compliance
Lightning Source LLC
LaVergne TN
LVHW020649100826
845148LV00012B/2403

"Our lives today are a marathon of stress, exhaustion, anxiety, and even despair. But within this heaviness, hope still gleams forth. *A Month of Comfort and Wisdom* reveals the source of that hope through quiet daily study of the Holy Scripture. Reach for these beautiful meditations—every day—to light a path through the wilderness and bring strength into these difficult days."

—Susan Sparks, preacher, comedian, author

"Dr. Hood is my pastor, but I like to kid him by calling him, 'coach.' Through these daily meditations, he coaches me to be a better disciple. The 'coach' through these meditations will strengthen your spirit and relationship with God. Enjoy coming to the practice field by reading this book so that you, too, can be part of God's team."

—Steve Anderson, school administrator, retired

"Perhaps the most comforting thing about this collection of ponderings and petitions is how near to my aching heart they draw. Thorne's prayers are accessible in a way that feels familiar, honest, and true; I easily lay them at the Lord's altar as my own."

—Lauren Lisa Ng, Senior Program Officer,
Berkeley School of Theology

"How many of us have had moments, or hours, or days, or months, during which we have felt the strong need for spiritual support and comfort, and didn't know where to turn? The authors of this small resource are trusted spiritual leaders providing comfort and wisdom as we navigate the challenges of life."

—Kenneth Janson, MD

"This collection of meditations is a divine gift, offering the guidance and wisdom needed to navigate life's journey with faith and grace."

—Barbara C. Sageman, executive leader in strategy,
fundraising, and team development

"*A Month of Comfort and Wisdom* arrives at a time when many seek reassurance and hope. This volume offers a daily practice of prayer and reflection, gently guiding readers toward God's comfort and wisdom. Each brief meditation begins with Scripture, inviting both mind and heart to open. Readers are encouraged to settle, reflect, and receive what they need most. Throughout, a consistent emphasis on humor and joy acts as a tonic, lightening the soul. These meditations serve as a roadmap to sustaining prayer, offering a connection to God's presence."

—Laurie Ferguson, Leadership Coach